Roosevelt Homes
of the Hudson Valley

ROOSEVELT HOMES
of the HUDSON VALLEY

Hyde Park and Beyond

SHANNON BUTLER

THE
History
PRESS

Published by The History Press
Charleston, SC
www.historypress.com

First published 2020

ISBN 9781540243850

Library of Congress Control Number: 2020938465

Dedicated to my family: Mom, Dad, Shawn, Rich and, even though he always had to be on my lap when I was working, to my little Mocha.

CONTENTS

CONTENTS

PREFACE

What does it mean to call a place home? Is it a place where you spend most of your time? Is it where you feel safe, warm and loved? Does it have to be a place where you live? Or can it be a place where you can connect with people and memories? Can it be a place where you've experienced intellectual, spiritual and overall personal growth? The fact is that it is possible for us to feel at home in many kinds of places. Our family home—where we grew up—can be a place to call our home base. Our school or college can also feel like home to those who enjoyed their time there. Our church or place of worship can be a spiritual home and can even bring additional family members. Our best friend's house could always be relied on as a place for comfort and good times. Visiting grandparents, aunts, uncles and other family members' houses could also feel like home. One thing is true for almost all of us: no matter where we are in life, no matter the levels of our responsibilities or our place in society, we long for a place that we can call home.

Now, imagine you are the leader of one of the most powerful nations on earth. You travel to different places every day. You attend meetings from the moment you wake until the moment you return to bed—perhaps it's not even the bed with which you are most familiar. Imagine, further still, you are the leader during one of our country's most trying times. Not only is the country still recovering from the Great Depression, but there are also racial tensions that seem to be getting worse. There is a massive war raging overseas with world leaders begging for your help. To top it off, your country has just been attacked, leading to the death of thousands of your people. Put yourself in the shoes of the thirty-second president of the United States, Franklin Delano Roosevelt. It's December 7, 1941, and your current residence is 1600 Pennsylvania Avenue, Washington, D.C. But is that home to you? Is there any other place you would rather be?

Imagine that you are in the shoes of First Lady Eleanor Roosevelt. It could be argued that it was even harder for her, as she had never really known a home of her own for most of her life. She, too, was looking for comfort while trying to fight for human rights and aid her husband's endeavor to win the war and save the nation. For FDR, there were several possibilities all over the country to which he could run away. But it's a body of water, and the several homes along it, that he and Eleanor turned to time and time again for comfort and solace.

FDR once said, "All that is within me cries out to go back to my home on the Hudson." He came back to his family's estate as often as he could—in good times and bad. The house he was born in changed over time in size and appearance, but it would always remain dear to him—so much so that not only did he use it to entertain some of the most prominent leaders of the mid-twentieth century, but he also decided to preserve it for future generations. The estate at Hyde Park contains much more than just the family's mansion and gardens. About two miles away from the main house is a cottage where Eleanor Roosevelt would spend much of her time. It was a place that inspired her work in social causes and her personal growth. Just up the hill from this little cottage is another cozy cottage of which FDR personally oversaw the design and construction. Top Cottage was essentially the "man cave" in the woods. This little house overlooked the valley that meant the world to FDR, and if you were invited here, it meant that the president wanted to show you more of who he really was.

Aside from the various houses that Franklin and Eleanor lived in, there were several other places along the Hudson that had meaning to them. Like many other socialite families, the Roosevelts had homes in New York City. It was common to spend the winter season in Manhattan and then take the train up the Hudson to the country. The townhouse on East Sixty-Fifth Street that was built by the president's mother, Sara Delano Roosevelt, was meant as a gift to her son and daughter-in-law. Eleanor Roosevelt was born in the city in a house that once stood on East Thirty-Seventh Street. Later in her life, the city was where she spent much of her time while working in the United Nations, and the townhouse where she passed away is still standing. Heading up the river, we come to Newburgh, where the president's mother was born and raised. Sara Delano Roosevelt was one of the key role models in FDR's life, and it is her family home, Algonac, where FDR spent many happy hours with cousins and his maternal grandparents.

Across the river and just north of Poughkeepsie, we find several Roosevelt-related sites. The Roosevelts' first country home, Mount Hope, is long gone, but across the street is Rosedale, where FDR's uncle and cousins lived. In the town of Hyde Park there are several Roosevelt-related residences, including the home of FDR's half-brother Rosy, the main estate Springwood and the site of FDR's spiritual home, St. James Church. Travel up Albany Post Road toward Rhinebeck, and we find several homes of family and friends, where FDR spent some of his free time. His cousin Laura Delano lived in a beautiful Tudor-style home, where FDR entertained Winston Churchill. Not far from there is the beautiful Wilderstein, the home of Daisy Suckley, a devoted confidant and distant cousin. Just north of the village of Rhinebeck is yet another Delano residence—the home of FDR's great-aunt and uncle Steen Valetje. This grand house was once part of the Astor family estate. If we venture to the border of Dutchess and Columbia Counties, we find the house where Eleanor spent many of her childhood years—not all of them pleasant.

When FDR began his political career as a New York state senator, much of his time was spent in Albany. There, the family rented homes and stayed on and off while Roosevelt developed his diplomatic reputation. Many years later, the family would take a new home, the Governor's Mansion, also known as the Executive Mansion. There, FDR used a therapy pool to deal with his physical issues while he worked out the problems of New York State.

It is believed that home is where the heart is, but it is so much more than that. To the members of the Hudson branch of the Roosevelt family, there were plenty of places where they could feel at ease during hard times. Let us take a journey from the mouth of the Hudson River in New York City and venture over one hundred miles north to discover the many places along the way that played a role in comforting and stimulating one of the most influential families of the twentieth century.

Acknowledgements

There are so many places that I have visited and conducted research at over the years, and I am sure there were other resources I didn't get the chance to encounter, but first, I have to acknowledge the National Park Service and the staff at the Roosevelt-Vanderbilt National Historic Site. I spent eight years working at Springwood, Val-Kill and Top Cottage among some very talented people and even had the chance to speak with several Roosevelt grandchildren over the years. I want to thank Franceska Macsali-Urbin, Frank Futral and Tara McGill for their help finding everything, from sources to photographs to good stories.

In my time as a park ranger, I had the chance, on several occasions, to sit down and talk with David Roosevelt, and he has always been kind and helpful to me over the years. Also, I want to thank Nina Roosevelt Gibson for the valuable information concerning some of Eleanor Roosevelt's employees at Val-Kill. Also, though sadly he has passed away, I am very grateful for the information that Curtis Roosevelt was willing to share with me back when I was a young park ranger and college student.

I must also thank the good folks at the Franklin D. Roosevelt Presidential Library and Museum. A special thanks to all of the archivists who have helped me over the years with all of my various research projects. FDR had the good sense to put everything that was important to him and his history in one place, for the most part, and I know I speak for many other Roosevelt historians when I say thanks to him.

I must also give a special thank-you to Duane and Linda Watson at Wilderstein Historic Site, who not only aided me with this book but also invited me into their collections as an intern many years ago. I am thankful to both of them for their guidance and friendship.

Thank you to Jonathon Simons for sharing your fabulous photos of Steen Valetje with me and allowing me to borrow some of them for this book.

When it comes to the governor sites in Albany, New York, nobody knows them better than Stuart Lehman. Stuart was very kind to not only give me a private tour of the Executive Mansion but also provide some helpful literature on the site.

Thank you to the people of Hyde Park, who continue to trust me with their history. Thank you to the people of St. James Episcopal Church, my spiritual home and family, just as it was for FDR.

A big thank-you goes out to my family, Mom, Dad, Shawn, Rich and Mocha, for always supporting me and putting up with my work—and sometimes my whining.

Part One

—— · ❧ · ——

NEW YORK CITY

Early Roosevelts

New York City has a history that stretches to the early Dutch settlers and to the Native Americans before that. The Roosevelt family could trace their connections to the city almost back to its beginning. By the time the small town of New Amsterdam began to thrive, the Roosevelts had managed to make a home for themselves right in the middle of it all. Claes Martenszen van Rosenvelt was the first of the family to venture from the Netherlands. Though the exact date is unclear, it was most likely in the 1640s when he made his home on the island of Manhattan. The original Roosevelt farm appears to have been located where the Empire State Building currently stands and comprised about fifty acres purchased from Lambert van Valckenburgh.[1] By the eighteenth century, FDR's great-great-grandfather Isaac Roosevelt had moved the family into the business of sugar. He was one of the first to build a sugar refinery on Wall Street and then moved to Queen Street, now known as Pearl Street, sometime around 1772.

FDR was incredibly proud of his family's history and heritage, particularly of the accomplishments of his great-great-grandfather Isaac. Isaac Roosevelt was born in 1726 in New York City. Not only did he make the family's fortune, but he also helped write the history of New York State. Isaac was nominated to serve in the Provincial Congress in April 1775.[2] He took part in the writing of New York's state constitution in 1777. After the Revolutionary War, he cofounded the Bank of New York along with friend and fellow Patriot Alexander Hamilton. Isaac married Cornelia Hoffman, whose family owned land in Dutchess County along the Hudson River, and it was there, along the banks of the river, that the Hyde Park branch of the Roosevelt family would eventually find their home. FDR's pride in his ancestors appeared at an early age, while attending Harvard, when he composed a thesis concerning the Roosevelts of New Netherland and the effects they had on the development of the colony. Later, he would show off his love for Isaac the Patriot by showcasing a portrait of him painted by Gilbert Stuart in the main living room of the family's house at Hyde Park.

Isaac spent the majority of his time in the city, but in 1752, he made his way up the river to marry his wife, Cornelia, in Rhinebeck and to serve with the state senate in Kingston in 1777. With the success of his sugar business and the wealth that came with his marriage into the Hoffman family, Isaac was able to send his son James to college at Princeton.

James Roosevelt, born in 1760, was part of the fifth generation of Roosevelts since Claes's immigration to America. He took after his father in the sugar refining business and banking. His residence was located at 18 South Street, where many gentlemen found themselves living very close to their respective businesses. In 1785, only a couple of years after the British occupation ended, Isaac managed to purchase land around the "Bowery lane and first street" of New York City; ironically, it's now the area known as Sara D. Roosevelt Park.[3] He also had a farm in what is now Harlem, which was customary at the time.

By the 1820s and '30s, many of these gentlemen found themselves in a sort of flight northward as more and more immigrants made their way into lower Manhattan, and eventually, James moved to 64 Bleecker Street between what is now Greenwich Village and East Village. This became his main residence in the city in his later years. Of course, nothing remains of any of the early Roosevelt residences in New York City. It is clear, however, that when Claes, Isaac, James and even FDR's father, also named James, lived here, much of what we now call the city was open land that would be farmed, altered, manicured, developed and redeveloped.

Delano Residence, Colonnade Row

One of the earliest residences that we can still find evidence of is from FDR's maternal side of the family, the Delanos. FDR's mother, the formidable Sara Delano Roosevelt, was convinced that her son was a Delano first and a Roosevelt second. Her family had roots in America going back even further than the Roosevelts, since Phillip Delano had made his way to Plymouth Colony in 1621. FDR's love of sailing ships and maritime history came from the stories of early family merchants like Ephraim Delano sailing along the coast of the colonies in the mid-eighteenth century. He also enjoyed hearing about Captain Warren Delano, who was captured by the British navy during the War of 1812—not once but twice. He loved hearing the stories of his mother, who, as a little girl, sailed to China with her mother and siblings to join her father, who was involved in his latest venture in the trade of tea and opium. It was this man, Warren Delano Jr., who would make the family immensely wealthy and was able to move them into some exquisite homes along the Hudson.

In 1846, Warren Delano Jr. was living in China with his wife, Catherine; their child, Louise; and his younger brother Edward, who had helped him with business. The brothers had both served in the large American firm Russell and Co., and Warren had been working in and out of China since first sailing there in 1833, when he was twenty-three. However, by 1846, Warren and his wife had lost one child, a daughter named Susan, from sickness; the business of opium trading was dangerous and destructive; and the desire to return home to America was weighing on the minds of everyone in the family. By this time, the Delano family had clearly established a fortune—certainly enough money to sustain a respectable lifestyle back home—so they all agreed to make their way back to the States.

The Delano family had settled in New England in the 1600s, and their main residence was still located in Fairhaven, Massachusettes, but Warren knew that the place to be for trade and potential growth in investments was New York City. It was also fashionable to have a home where one could be seen among some of the most elite families in society. Warren moved the family into an elaborate townhouse at LaGrange Terrace on Lafayette Street, next to his other younger brother Franklin Hughes Delano, who had married Laura Astor a few years before. They had many famous neighbors, including the Vanderbilts, Astors and Washington Irving, living next door in this luxurious complex of buildings now known as Colonnade Row.[4]

This Greek Revival building is said to have been the work of Hudson River architect Andrew Jackson Downing, though other architects have also been credited for its design. The row originally contained nine townhouses built between 1830 and 1832 by Seth Geer. The twenty-seven-foot-wide houses connected to one another, and each contained twenty-six rooms. The front of each house was linked with Corinthian columns made of Westchester marble that was quarried by prisoners at Sing Sing. The design is considered to be borrowed from the British row enclaves of the 1830s.

Laura Astor Delano kept excellent records concerning the day-to-day needs of the household for her and Franklin Hughes Delano at LaGrange Terrace. In 1845, she hired a cook named Catharine Foley at "$9 a month," and "Ellen Webb came as a chambermaid at $7 a month." Mrs. Higgins would come and clean the house for $5.00, and a man named Dean brought ice to the house quite regularly. She wrote everything from daily purchases, like butter and eggs, to fancier items, like oysters, Madeira nuts and brandy peaches. She must have been preparing for a small party on October 14, 1845, when she paid $3.87 for tea, ice cream, grapes and coconut cake. She would also record when her husband gave her money, and how much, to pay for these various needs and wages. He usually gave her about $100.00 a month, which would be nearly $3,000.00 today, occasionally adding more if there was a need.[5] We can see that Franklin also wished to have a fine instrument for their home when he ordered a rosewood pianoforte manufactured by Chickering and Mackay's in Boston for $375.00.

In Warren Delano's personal accounts, we find that he had an insurance policy on his new residence worth $10,000.00 a year. On the other hand, he paid someone $0.01 per month to store the thirty-two cases of Madeira wine

Colonnade Row, Lafayette Square below Astor Place, 1890. By Robert L. Bracklow. *From the collections of the Museum of the City of New York.*

that he had imported from Canton, China, in 1841. Like his brother, he also ordered a fine pianoforte for his residence. From furniture maker George Platt in New York City, he ordered a mahogany bookcase, a pair of Louise XIV pedestals with marble tops and walnut bookcases with glass doors, all at a sum of $390.00. The 1840s was a time of modern advancements, and Warren wished to have new plumbing installed in the house, which included a new bathing tub, water closet, waste and soil pipes and a fifty-two-gallon steam boiler at a cost of about $275.00.[6] There was a need for fresh paint on all of the floors of the house, including details in the parlors and the main entry hall, which came out to about $564.00.

Based on the financial records of the family, it was no small feat to keep and maintain this house for any of the Delanos. However, Eleanor Roosevelt would later write in her autobiography that "the Delanos were the first people I met who were able to do what they wanted to do without wondering where to obtain the money."[7]

Colonnade Row was exactly the sort of residence—in the perfect neighborhood and with the most recognizable neighbors—that Warren needed to sustain his family's place in New York society. That his wealth had been made by taking advantage of the opium crisis in China didn't seem to bother anyone. John Jacob Astor had also taken part in that venture, and both men lived in a time when questionable business deals were likely to be ignored if conducted by those of high birth. The money they made in silks, china and tea was quite enough to sustain their new lifestyles of elegance. It should be noted that the Delano family, with the help of their wealth, also contributed to New York society by building a free hospital for children by 1884. At a cost of about $150,000, the Laura Franklin Hospital was named for their daughter, who tragically burned to death in a freak accident in 1884.

As for Colonnade Row today, there are only four buildings still remaining of the original nine. Numbers 428, 430, 432 and 434 were some of the earliest buildings to be added to the New York City Landmarks, which began in 1965. They are also in the National Register of Historic Places, as of 1976. Though the buildings have been altered somewhat and split into various apartments and businesses, the strong and tall Corinthian columns that made them stand out in the 1830s are just as important and unique in our modern times. It is lovely to imagine the sounds of a pianoforte playing and the sights of the Delano men and women sitting in their finery enjoying their tea, cake and Madeira wine.

Eleanor Roosevelt's Childhood Homes

The two most famous Roosevelts born in New York City are Theodore Roosevelt, who went on to become president, and Eleanor Roosevelt, who history would refer to as the "first lady of the world." Theodore is part of the Oyster Bay branch of the family, as they would later be known, thanks to the home he called Sagamore Hill that he built in that part of Long Island. Eleanor was both a Hyde Park and an Oyster Bay Roosevelt, as she was the daughter of Theodore's little brother Elliott and then married into the Hyde Park branch. As a child, she spent time visiting with her Oyster Bay cousins and remembered trying to keep up with her uncle on morning runs to the beach, where the water, and the idea of jumping in with the rest of the family, always frightened her.

Eleanor was born on October 11, 1884, at 56 West Thirty-Seventh Street. She was the first child of Anna Hall Roosevelt and Elliott Roosevelt. The world that she came into was a joyous one at first. Her parents were considered to be society's most beautiful and delightful pair. They attended all of the most elegant parties and sporting events. They were talked about in all of the social papers and clubs. Elliott was the younger brother of Theodore Roosevelt, and he made a modest living working at one of the leading real estate firms of New York, the Ludlow firm. Anna was a descendent of the Livingston family on her mother's side, and her grandfather Edward Ludlow had made a fortune in New York real estate and started the firm where Elliott worked. Eleanor's arrival was a bit of a disappointment, as her parents were hoping for a

Portrait of Eleanor Roosevelt taken in New York, 1889. *Franklin D. Roosevelt Library and Museum.*

son. Eleanor was not considered to be as beautiful as her mother, which appeared to concern, at least, Anna, who called her "Granny." Elliott, on the other hand, adored his little "Nell" and showed her the love and attention she desired.

Eleanor's childhood was spent in several different places, and the house on Thirty-Seventh Street was more of a resting point between her family's many retreats on Long Island and Newport. Sometimes she was sent away with her various Roosevelt and Hall relatives when her parents traveled abroad.

Anna soon gave birth to two boys. First was Elliott Jr. in 1889, followed by Gracie Hall in 1891, while the family was in Europe. By this time, things were beginning to unravel for the happy couple. Elliott's love of sports and drinking had led to several accidents that caused him to break first a collarbone and then a leg, which would be a continual source of great pain. He took to self-medication with the use of laudanum mixed with increasingly heavy drinking. Just after the birth of their second son, Anna decided that her husband was a danger to her and the children. The time they were spending in Europe, which she had hoped would be the source of a cure for Elliott's illness, was proving more painful than anticipated. Anna made the decision to bring the children back to the United States and officially separated from her husband.

Anna and the children moved into 52 East Sixty-First Street to be away from her husband, but Eleanor began to spend more time with her grandmother Mary Livingston Ludlow Hall, who had a house at number 11 West Thirty-Seventh Street as well as an old home up the Hudson River in Tivoli. While Eleanor was living with her maternal relatives, she secretly longed to be with her father, who by 1892 had made his way to the home of his brother-in-law Douglas Robinson, who had property in Southwest Virginia. The hope was that the work on that estate would keep Elliott out of trouble. Meanwhile, Anna's relatives were worried about young Eleanor's lack of education. Eleanor's great-aunt Margaret Livingston Ludlow, also known as Aunt Maggie, helped set up a teacher for her while her mother was suffering from poor health.[8]

Sadly, not long after enduring an operation, in late November 1892, Anna was diagnosed with diphtheria and died soon after at the age of twenty-nine on December 7.[9] Eleanor later admitted that she did not mourn the loss of her mother; instead, she was happy to know that her father would be coming back to New York. The funeral for Anna was held in her home on 61st Street, and from there, Eleanor and her little brothers were sent to live with Grandmother Hall on West 37th Street. It was in this house that Eleanor would be briefly reunited with her father for a short moment. As she recalled in her autobiography, her father was sitting in a big chair and looked very sad all dressed in black. Over the course of the next year, her brother Elliott died from diphtheria, which had developed just after he contracted scarlet fever. Her father, overcome with grief and still dealing with his own demons, tried to commit suicide but failed, only to die a few days later on August 14, 1894, in his residence at number 313 West 102nd Street.

Life after the loss of her father was melancholy, as Eleanor explained in her autobiography. Her grandmother's house in the city was very much like all of the other brownstone houses on the outside. Inside, it was a dark place where everything seemed to make her uncomfortable. Her grandmother was not able to control her own children, who grew up undisciplined, so she was determined to see to it that Eleanor and Hall were taught to follow the rules.[10]

Eleanor did not write much more about her young life in these houses in New York City, as most of the first decade of her life was spent in sadness and discomfort. Many of these old brownstone homes where Eleanor's early life took place are long gone, and more modern construction has taken their places.

Eleanor and Franklin's Early New York City Residences

Eleanor Roosevelt spent a good deal of her time living between West Thirty-Seventh Street and Tivoli after the death of her parents. In 1899, she was shipped off to England to receive a proper education. She was fifteen years old when she entered a finishing school many of her relatives had attended, the Allenswood Boarding Academy for girls. She recalled the few years she spent abroad as some of her happiest. With her head teacher, Mademoiselle Souvestre, she traveled across Europe and found confidence that she never previously had.

She returned to New York in the summer of 1903 because her grandmother insisted that she enter society, which was what all teenage girls did in her class. She moved in with her cousin Susan Parish, who lived at 8 East Seventy-Sixth Street. This was part of a lovely building, and her great-uncle and aunt Edward and Margaret Livingston Ludlow lived next door at number 6. In 1895, the Ludlows had commissioned the architectural firm of Parish & Schroeder to design two side-by-side homes. Essentially, there are two houses as mirror images on the inside, and the outside is a single Italian Renaissance palazzo. The separate entrances were disguised by a single portico supported by paired columns, and the exterior is lined with beige brick and limestone. It is not as elaborate as some of the other homes built in that era and in that part of the city, but it soon housed some of society's big revelries.

During one of her various train trips along the Hudson, Eleanor ran into her fifth cousin once removed, Franklin Delano Roosevelt. They began to spend more time together, especially during her trips to Groton to visit her brother Hall, who was studying there. It was during one of these trips in the fall of 1903 that Franklin asked his nineteen-year-old distant cousin to marry him.[11] The proposal shocked many in the family. Eleanor said yes before she even understood the meaning of love and whether she actually was in love. History shows us that Eleanor and Franklin were made to wait due to Franklin's mother and her concerns that the two of them were too young to marry. Perhaps Sara Delano Roosevelt hoped that her boy would change his mind, but he did not.

There are no known photographs of the wedding or the decorated scene. Instead, there are written accounts from Eleanor and relatives, who showered more attention on the bride's uncle, President Theodore Roosevelt, than the soon-to-be-married couple. Plans were set for the wedding to be on St. Patrick's Day, since the president would be in town that day for the parade.

With the early death of her father, it became Uncle Theodore's job to give Eleanor away. All festivities were to be held at the house on East Seventy-Sixth Street, where Eleanor had been living, because it was big enough to hold both the ceremony and the lunch. Susan Parish's drawing room opened into her mother, Mrs. Ludlow's side. An altar was prepared near the fireplace, and the *New York Times* wrote, "The two large drawing rooms on the second floor, done alike in pale amber-yellow satin brocade, were thrown into one large salon running the width of the two houses."

The *Los Angeles Herald* wrote, "A huge floral cluster of 1,000 pink roses, entwined with smilax and asparagus, was suspended in the center of the drawing room and formed a canopy."

After Mr. and Mrs. Ludlow passed away, their side of the house was sold. Susan Parish lived on her side of the house for half a century, and she was a frequent visitor to the White House when Eleanor and Franklin moved there. After her death in 1950, her side was sold the following year. The lovely townhouse on East Seventy-Sixth Street still stands to this day, though the downstairs has been turned into doctors' offices and the upper floors have been broken up into luxury apartments. From the outside, there is no way of knowing that this was the site of a famous wedding that the president of the United States pushed his way through streets filled with parade goers and spectators just to make it to.

After the wedding, Eleanor and Franklin went to Hyde Park before preparing for their overseas honeymoon. They spent the summer of 1905 visiting parts of England, Scotland, Paris, Venice and Switzerland. While they were abroad, they considered where they might make a home for themselves in New York City. They relied on Sara to find them a suitable place. They were both interested in a house located just a few blocks from where his mother had been living on Madison, 125 East Thirty-Sixth Street. Franklin wrote his mother, informing her of their desire to have the house: "Our one hope is to hear very soon that you have got it for us." He continued, "It would be so nice to feel that all is settled before we return."[12] Sara not only managed to rent them the house that they wanted for two years, but she also prepared the house for their arrival, complete with servants. It was in this "fourteen-foot mansion," as they called it, that the first two of their children were born—Anna in May 1906 and James in December 1907. The house still stands today with a small plaque near the door that tells of its brief Roosevelt connection.

Even though Sara had managed to get them the house they desired, it was not what she wanted for them. She informed the two newlyweds only months after they had moved into their little townhouse that she had a bigger home in mind—one they could share. During Christmas 1905, on a piece of Hyde Park letterhead, she scribbled a little drawing of a townhouse that she was planning. "A Christmas Present to Franklin and Eleanor from Mama," she wrote below the drawing, "number and street not yet quite decided—19 or 20 feet wide." She even scribbled a little cloud of smoke coming from the chimney, as if the home were already built and lived in.

She purchased the plot of land between Park and Madison Avenues, which had two brownstones still standing. That part of town was rapidly becoming a fashionable place to live, and she paid a good deal of money for the property, $79,000. The two homes that had been built in 1876 were going out of style by the twentieth century. The fashion of the brownstone was being replaced with the Beaux-Arts château as the wealthy were beginning to build their grand palaces in the style of the French. Sara made the decision to demolish the two houses and build something that better represented her family's place in old money society and celebrated their long and rich heritage. The Roosevelts were one of the first families in the area to start the trend of taking down the old style and building something new.

Sara's next job was to find the right architect. The man she chose, architect Charles A. Platt, was involved in remodeling the Astor estate at the time. Platt was educated in New York City and started out as an artist and sketcher. He made his way into a career in landscape design in the 1890s. By the beginning of the twentieth century, Platt was well known for his country estates and gardens. Sara hired him, in part, because of his connections through his work with the Astors.[13]

Number 125 East Thirty-Sixth Street, also known as the fourteen-foot mansion. *Franklin D. Roosevelt Library and Museum.*

Platt started drawing up the plans for the house in 1906. While the new money families, like the Vanderbilts, were building grand châteaux along Fifth Avenue, the old money families, like the Roosevelts, preferred a simpler, elegant style. Platt designed one large building that contains two houses that are mirror images of each other. The exterior of the home looks like one grand house, but on entering the front door, one enters a hall with a door on the left for number 47, the home of Sara Delano Roosevelt, and a door on the right for number 49, Eleanor and Franklin's residence. In these two houses, history was made time and time again.

The house itself stands strong with just a hint of elegance. It is thirty-five feet wide and sixty-eight feet deep. The exterior is of a Colonial Revival/Neo-Georgian style with buff brick and limestone trim. The Roosevelts, ever proud of their Dutch heritage, added a shield between the third and fourth floors with the family's crest of roses. The first floor and basement are made of limestone, with a large window on either side of the entranceway. This entire limestone level gives the impression of a base that the rest of the house is sitting on. The upper levels of the house are constructed of light brown buff brick, with sixteen large windows trimmed in limestone. The entrance is an archway of limestone, complete with an iron fanlight above the doors, which are likewise made of hand-forged iron. Between the first and second floors, there is a small iron balcony going the length of the entrance façade. There are also rows of limestone trim between the second and third floors and the fourth and fifth, almost giving the look of an elegant layer cake. The house is similar in design to the exterior of Platt's other East Sixty-Fifth Street house, number 125, the home of Frederick S. Lee, which Platt designed a year or two earlier and the Roosevelts had very much admired.

Platt designed the house to be two mirror houses connected, just as Sara had seen in the Ludlow houses, where Franklin and Eleanor had been married. On the first floor, the homes have an entrance hall or sitting room as well as matching stairwells, bathrooms and elevators. In the rear of the houses are the dining rooms with a large connecting doorway that allows them to combine into one great hall. Eleanor wrote in her autobiography in later years, "The houses were narrow but made the most of every inch of space and built them so that the dining rooms and drawing rooms could be thrown together and made practically one big room."[14] The problem was that this allowed her domineering mother-in-law access to every part of the house whenever she liked. Eleanor showed her dislike of this feature. In her later years, she said, "You were never quite sure when she would appear, day or night." However, as the family grew and Eleanor and Franklin had five children, it would prove quite useful to allow the children more room to run between the two houses, as well as having Sara there to keep an eye on them.

The second floors had matching libraries at the front of the houses and drawing rooms in the rear, while the third and fourth floors had bedrooms

View of East Sixty-Fifth Street, designed by Charles A. Platt. *Photo taken by the author.*

for the families. The fifth and sixth floors were bedrooms for the servants, and the roof was an area the servants used to dry laundry. In the basement level, there was a coal burner, a kitchen and pantry area for the servants, as well as their own dining hall. Beginning on the third floor, between the two houses is a courtyard that goes up to the roof with a large sunlight. This allows light to flow through the houses. There are large windows on the rest of the floors in the interior of the light court. The total cost between land purchase, demolition of the old brownstones, construction and architect's fee ended up being $247,000.

With the building of the Roosevelts' new home, the area surrounding the townhouse would very quickly start to change. The look of East Sixty-Fifth Street, in particular, evolved from the old brownstone row houses to the refined townhouses that reflected the influence of the Beaux-Arts movement. As the area around Park Avenue became more fashionable, the blocks around it followed this architectural trend. The Upper East Side Historic District Designation Report of 1981 claims that the Roosevelt house, along with others nearby, "in these styles are among the finest in the City."[15] This house proved to be a great source of pride for Sara, but Eleanor, sadly, never grew to love it.

It was in this home that Eleanor discovered the heartbreaking letters that proved her husband had been unfaithful in 1918. She was unpacking his luggage upstairs in their room as Franklin recovered from his trip overseas during the war. There, she found the love letters between him and Lucy Mercer, a former social secretary.[16]

A few years later, when FDR contracted polio in 1921, he came to this house to be close to New York City's best physicians. He recuperated in his bedroom on the third floor, while Eleanor pressed ahead with the help of political aide Louis Howe to keep FDR's name alive in politics. Since he was unable to walk and was confined to a wheelchair in the early stages of the illness, FDR took advantage of the electric elevators that his mother had installed in both of the houses, as it was impossible for him to make his way up the stairs until he built up the strength in his upper body. During the next seven years, there would be a nonstop army of reporters, politicians, friends and family who would come and go both to wish him well and press him back into the political race.

He started his campaign to run for governor of New York State in this house. He also began his race for the presidency in this house. When he won forty-two out of the forty-eight states in 1932, it was in this house that he got the news that he would be moving to Washington.

During the presidential years, the house was lived in by some of FDR's children. His daughter Anna and her husband, Curtis Dall, moved in with Sara on her side of the house when they fell on rough times during the Great Depression. His son James and his wife, Betsey Cushing, used the

Steps of East Sixty-Fifth Street, showing the special railing for FDR. *Franklin D. Roosevelt Library and Museum.*

house briefly during the 1930s. Eleanor preferred to live in an apartment in Greenwich Village for the most part to avoid the folly of the press, until Sara's health began to decline in the late 1930s. Eleanor returned to the house to tend to her ailing mother-in-law from time to time. When Sara Delano Roosevelt died on September 7, 1941, the Roosevelts decided it was time to sell their home in Manhattan. A for sale sign was hung outside the house by September 16, 1941. It took Eleanor several months to clear out both of the houses.

When the war started a few months later, the real estate market in New York suffered, and even though the family was asking only $60,000 for the house, they would not find a buyer quickly. The president of Hunter College, Dr. George N. Shuster, expressed his interest in purchasing the home and using it as a student center for the college. FDR offered to lower the price to $50,000 and contribute $1,000 toward the sale of the house in his mother's name. By June 1942, Eleanor was attending the opening ceremony of the new center after the school had hired Shreve, Lamb, and Harmon to get the house ready for professional use. They tore down the walls that separated the dining rooms and drawing rooms to connect them into usable classrooms. But the overall look and layout of the building remained intact.[17]

For nearly half a century, the house was used by Hunter College for meetings, lectures and even weddings of college students. Eleanor continued to be involved with the college and the Roosevelt house until her death in 1962. She was constantly concerned with the education of the young people of this country and took great pride in the diversity and opportunity that the college offered.

The house was designated a New York City landmark by 1973 and was placed in the National Register of Historic Places by 1980. After years of constant use, the house fell into disrepair, and by 1992, the college was forced to close it for a series of renovations. By 2005, the restoration began when the college hired architect James Stewart Polshek to not only restore but also redesign the house for a new era of education. Now the house could serve as an example of repurposing historic buildings, which became a popular trend in the city in the 1960s.

When the project began, Polshek had high hopes. "It was really decayed and yet the bones were still good," he said in an interview after its completion. He began by demolishing the old walls between the two houses, making it one building that is thirty-five feet wide. He then rebuilt the wall with better access between both sides to follow modern building codes. The decision was made to build an auditorium in the rear of the house in its lower levels that could serve as a lecture hall and classroom, complete with state-of-the-art lighting, projection and sound systems. The servants' space in the basement has become gallery space for artwork and exhibits. The dining rooms are now one large parlor with doors that lead out to a terrace that sits on top of the auditorium. The second and third floors have classrooms and libraries for study, and the top floors are used as offices for college faculty and bedrooms for visiting scholars. The project was completed in 2010 at a total cost of around $24 million. Today, the building is still in the hands of Hunter College and is known as the Roosevelt House Public Policy Institute.[18]

Hunter College continues to uphold the legacy of the Roosevelts and their goals toward human rights equality and the education of young people. This house is a reminder of not only great New York City architecture but also of the powerful people who used this city as a base of operation during unprecedented times and circumstances. The Roosevelts used this house and this city for great inspiration over half a century ago, and today, our leaders of tomorrow are doing the same.

ELEANOR ROOSEVELT'S LAST CITY HOME,
55 EAST SEVENTY-FOURTH STREET

B y the 1930s, the dynamics of Eleanor and Franklin's marriage had changed so drastically that they were living separately most of the time. Franklin's affair with Lucy Mercer in 1918 had taken its toll on the marriage. After 1924, Franklin spent much of the year in Warm Springs, Georgia, where he swam in the warm mineral waters for his health. Meanwhile, Eleanor befriended new political associates like Louis Howe, Marian Dickerman, Nancy Cook, Ester Lape and Elizabeth Read, who worked with her to keep FDR's name alive in politics. Franklin and Eleanor had their own separate political pursuits, friends, activities and, over time, residences.

Eleanor discovered that she was very comfortable spending time in Greenwich Village with Ester Lape and her partner, Elizabeth Read. In 1935, the couple convinced Eleanor that she should rent an apartment in their building at 20 East Eleventh Street. If you walk up to the five-story brick house today, you will find a plaque near the door that says Eleanor lived here from 1932 until 1942. She had the third-floor apartment, and Eleanor Roosevelt historian Blanche Wiesen Cook referred to the house as her New York City "sanctuary," where she could get away from the press, her mother-in-law and some of the madness that came with being the first lady.[19] After the death of Sara Delano Roosevelt and the sale of the East Sixty-Fifth Street house, Eleanor moved her family's New York City belongings into a new home at 29 Washington Square. She and Franklin signed a four-year lease in 1942 for a seven-room apartment, number

15a.[20] During their busy traveling schedule, this residence became more of a rest stop between Hyde Park and Washington.

Eleanor continued to live at this location after FDR's death in April 1945. By December 1949, she had moved on and was renting suites in the Park Sheraton Hotel at 202 West Fifty-Sixth Street, which she seemed to enjoy. "Yesterday we moved from Washington Square to the Park Sheraton Hotel," she wrote in her My Day column in 1949. She loved the view of Central Park and said, "I also can see the George Washington Bridge in the distance. It is beautiful during the day and like a fairyland when the lights come on."[21] The only problem she apparently had with the hotel was the scene of naked mermaids painted on the ceiling. However, by 1953, she wished for a place to set up house in the city, as well as a place to have her dogs with her. In September 1953, she moved to a house at 211 East Sixty-Second Street. An added bonus, which she was excited to tell the world about in her column, was that she also had a garden here.[22]

This house was just one in a series of buildings designed by M.C. Merritt in 1873 for Thomas Kilpatrick. Each building cost only $13,000 to build.[23] The area where the house is located is known as the Treadwell Farm Historic District, named for the family who owned the land since 1815, long before it was developed. Many of the houses that still stand here today were built between the late 1860s and 1870s. Other prominent architects in this district included Richard Morris Hunt and James W. Pirrson. The house still has some of its original features, including a beautifully curved stairway, wood fireplaces and leaded glass windows. Today, the house is meant for a single family, but when Eleanor lived here, it was cut into apartments.

During her stay, she hosted several dinner parties, where she discussed politics with leaders from all over the world. She continued to work on her famous My Day column, and in 1956, she helped support Adlai Stevenson in his run for the presidency from this home.[24]

Eleanor's good friend the Reverend William Turner Levy wrote about his many visits to Eleanor's apartments in the city in his book *The Extraordinary Mrs. R.* He mentioned being in the East Sixty-Second Street place, having drinks with Eleanor's son Elliott Roosevelt, when he noticed everything in the home reflected who Eleanor was. "A table, whose base was a handsome carved wooden elephant, bespoke the regard of peoples half a world away," he wrote, "and the four sunlight drenched watercolors by Louis Howe kept a loyal friend's memory incandescently present."[25]

She stayed here until the rent was increased before her lease ended in 1958. She had been wanting to move into a slightly bigger place, but in the meantime, she moved back to the Park Sheraton Hotel before settling in her final New York City residence.

Eleanor had befriended several couples who had inspired her choices of residences during the course of her life. The last place she called home in New York City was the suggestion of Edna and Dr. David Gurewitsch, who Eleanor cherished as friends. Dr. David met Eleanor in 1944, when he served as a doctor for her friend Trude Lash. Later, he became Eleanor's official physician. She insisted that she was quite healthy and would not take up too much of his time. Little did he know they would be spending a good deal of time together as friends. They traveled together quite frequently, and Gurewitsch, a talented photographer, documented their journeys with several detailed photographs that reveal Eleanor's passion for humanity and culture.

By 1958, he had married his new love, Edna Perkel, in Eleanor's apartment. Though Eleanor was somewhat dismayed to have lost her companion at first, she soon treated Edna as an additional companion, and they traveled all over the world and formed a tight bond of friendship. It was Edna who mentioned the possibility of the three sharing a townhouse together that would give Eleanor more room to work and David space to see patients. Edna searched the city for just the place to fit their needs, while Eleanor continued to stay at the Park Sheraton. "It is nice to be out of a hotel and in my own home again," Eleanor wrote in her My Day column on December 2, 1959, "though everyone in the Park Sheraton Hotel was so kind and considerate that I feel I owe them a debt of gratitude."[26]

By that point, she had spent a few nights in her portion of number 55 East Seventy-Fourth Street after a very quick move-in day, in which Edna Gurewitsch said, "Every preplanned detail was efficiently executed."[27]

The townhouse was one of eight limestone buildings designed in 1889 by the architectural partnership of Buchman and Deisler. It's a Neo-Renaissance style with Greek columns at the front entrance and an iron grille door. In the main entry hall is a marble floor and a sweeping, curved staircase leading to the upper floors. Eleanor decorated her portion of the house like she had decorated her other places—with lots of pictures and meaningful objects but never anything too extravagant. "Each picture, photograph, and object either meant something special to her or was of practical use," wrote Edna about Eleanor's decorating style.[28]

Some of Eleanor's photos on display in her apartment at 55 East Seventy-Fourth Street. *Franklin D. Roosevelt Library and Museum.*

The Gurewitsches lived on the fourth and fifth floors, while Eleanor had the lower floors. Together, the three could afford such a fine house due to their various careers. David was a successful doctor; Edna worked for Silberman Art Galleries, where she bought and sold fine art; and Eleanor was doing quite well making close to $90,000 a year writing for *McCall's Magazine*, writing her column My Day and being paid handsomely for her lectures.[29] Though they lived mostly separately in the house, the couple and Eleanor would sometimes share dinner in Eleanor's apartment before heading out to see a concert or play.

Eleanor could come and go easily between her residences in New York City and Hyde Park. In 1961, she wrote in her My Day column, "My home

Eleanor's bed, where she passed away in her apartment at 55 East Seventy-Fourth Street. *Franklin D. Roosevelt Library and Museum.*

and place where I vote is Hyde Park, N.Y., but much of my work is in the city and it is a second home."

But for a second home, Eleanor found herself busy in the final years that she spent there, as her schedule was packed with meetings, interviews and more writing projects. She sat down with her friend Reverend William Turner Levy to inform him that she had every intention of using what time she had left and that she had the strange blessing of knowing just how much time she had to spare: "Dr. Gurewitsch has told me that I have two years to live. It's a blood problem that involves the bone marrow."[30]

In the course of her life, she would produce over two dozen books and over seven thousand My Day columns, serve on countless committees and, to put it simply, she would be one of the most famous individuals of the twentieth century. Even until her last year of life, she worked tirelessly on her final book, *Tomorrow Is Now*, which would be her final plea to the youth of the nation to learn from both the mistakes and the messages of the past and carry on the fight for human and civil rights.[31] On November 7, 1962, Eleanor passed away in her bed at the townhouse she shared with the Gurewitsches. Over the years, the house has had many owners, as well as changes to the interior, and as of February 2020, the house was back on the market for $20 million.

Part Two

— · ✿ · —

MID-HUDSON REGION

DELANO HOME, ALGONAC

If you sail up the Hudson from New York City, you'll pass the beautiful Palisades region to the west. The cliffs rise high above the Hudson's edge and seem to go on for a long time. Farther upriver are West Point and the Highlands. There are remnants of Revolutionary War forts along the way. The river makes a sharp turn just below Newburgh, and to the north of the city, on the hill that overlooks the river, sits the home of Warren Delano. Newburgh was a town on the rise in the 1850s. It didn't have the noise and stuffiness of New York City, but it did have industry, commerce and elegant architecture blending together to form a desirable place to live. It also had easy access to the big city via steamboats and trains along the Hudson, so one could easily return to business after a visit to the country home. This was the dream of so many young businessmen with growing families, and Warren Delano set out to accomplish it in 1850.

As we saw earlier in New York City, the Delano family had made a home for themselves at the famous Colonnade Row. By the 1840s, Warren Delano had established his fortune and was inspired by his brother Franklin H. Delano, whose home was on the Astor estate farther upriver, to find a place of his own. Warren began to write to his brother for assistance in finding a proper house along the river's edge. At first, he could not find a suitable property to buy, so his next best option was to rent. Warren found a house just north of Newburgh, known as the Armstrong Mansion, in a place called Danskammer, which is Dutch for the "Devil's Dance Chamber." Warren loved this estate because of its beautiful granite house designed in the style of Maison Carre of Nimes, France, and the nine hundred acres that it sat on along the river.[32] However, he could not purchase the property. Today, it is the site of the Danskammer Generating Station, but from 1847 until 1851, the Delanos rented it while they continued to search for a place to call their own.

Warren wrote to his brother Franklin frequently, asking him to look into properties for him. In one letter, he wrote, "Fred met Cambridge Livingston the other day and was told by him that the Soler place is for sale 180 acres with good house and farm buildings for something between $20,000 and $25,000. If you have time to drive up and look on and around the place and examine a little the buildings and ascertain if and for what it can be bought I wish you would do so and let me know what you think of it."[33]

In 1851, he wrote to his brother again, this time considering the Higginson farm, which was between the house his family was renting and Newburgh, just east of the historic Balmville Tree. "By and by I shall try to send you a sketch of the Higginson grounds & house and before the end of the month, I shall probably know what chance of buying the Elliott portion which is desirable."[34] Not long after writing this letter, Warren purchased the Higginson farm, and work began to improve the estate with the help of some of the best architectural minds of the day.

Right from the beginning, Warren was concerned with the size of his new estate: "I have no immediate prospect of being able to buy any of the neighboring ground at a reasonable price and I fear I shall be confined to my original 50 or 52 acres which are not in all respects in a satisfactory shape." He temporarily named the estate Petite Place on account of its size, but Warren got right to work making it a home, regardless of how tiny it was. He continued in the letter, "I have four men now at work there cutting and getting the hay of which there may be 30 tons or more. There are many of the best varieties of cherries now ripening on the place and there is promise of a large crop of peaches, pears and quinces of the best kind." Warren went on to explain to his brother how fortunate he was to have Andrew Jackson Downing and Calvert Vaux working on plans to improve the house with additions, as well as barns, stables and a gatehouse.[35]

These letters between the Delano brothers show that Andrew Jackson Downing, a Newburgh native, and the English-born Calvert Vaux both had their talents involved in the creation of what ended up being named Algonac. They greatly improved the landscape and the house, which was redesigned by Downing in the Italian style, also referred to as Hudson Valley Bracketed. Downing had grown up in a little cottage overlooking the Hudson not far

Algonac in Newburgh, New York, 1888. Warren Delano is seen sitting in a wheelchair. *Franklin D. Roosevelt Library and Museum.*

from the home he was crafting for the Delanos, and he was well aware of how to take advantage of the scenery and landscape in his construction.[36] Algonac had several overhanging eaves and verandahs with sweeping views looking out on the Newburgh Bay and across the river to the Highlands. Downing finished his work at Algonac in 1852, not long before his untimely death on board the *Henry Clay*, a steamboat that caught fire near Riverdale, New York, on July 28, 1852.

The new home could boast being one of the grandest in the area, with forty rooms in total. On entry into the main hall, one could take a left and walk into a large drawing room "with a bay that looked out over the sunset."[37] It had a lovely library and dining room, and throughout the entire house, one could see that the family had spent many years abroad, particularly in China. Many pieces of furniture were made of teakwood. There were beautiful Chinese porcelain vases in several different sizes and paintings of Chinese merchants with whom Warren had once done

Algonac's gatehouse, which is still standing today. *Franklin D. Roosevelt Library and Museum.*

business. There were silk screens and pieces of carved jade that filled the cabinets and lined the bookshelves. It was a house of elegance and art, but first and foremost, it was a home that the Delano family would return to time and time again.

The property was a small functioning farm with gardens, trees of various types and orchards with fresh fruits. There were plenty of domestic animals on the farm, including horses, cows and plenty of dogs. There was a decent-size staff of devoted employees who, in many cases, lived and worked on the estate for most of their lives, including John Baird, who was the greenhouse keeper for more than fifty years. Peter Mahon managed to work his way up to the position of head chauffeur when he married the coachman's daughter. He also stayed with the family for nearly forty years.[38]

In 1931, Frederic Delano wrote a brief history of the family home on the eightieth anniversary of its creation. The house had moments of joy and pain, which were well documented in family diaries. It was here that Sara Delano was born on September 21, 1854. The family usually referred to her as Sallie. Sara married James Roosevelt in a small ceremony at Algonac on October 7, 1880.[39]

Inside the parlor at Algonac, filled with treasures from China. *Franklin D. Roosevelt Library and Museum.*

Sadly, some of the children and grandchildren of Warren and Catherine would die in this home as well. In December 1881, Philippe Delano passed away rather suddenly in the house. Just a month later, in January 1882, Warren III and Jennie's son Warren died after a terrible seizure of diphtheria and scarlet fever.[40] It was the death of this poor little boy that caused Sara to name her son Franklin Delano Roosevelt, instead of Warren, as she had originally planned. On July 20, 1884, someone in the family took the time to write, in horrible detail, the accidental death of Laura Delano, the youngest daughter. "At 9 o'clock an explosion as of a pistol, followed by an agonized shriek startled us all and immediately our darling child Laura flashed down the stairway a cloud of fiery flame." Laura had been curling her hair with a curling iron and had knocked over a lamp, which ignited her dressing gown. Dr. Ely arrived and proceeded to bandage her wounds while applying chloroform and morphine. The last line on the page reads, "3 o'clock in the morning the darling child drew her last breath and her sweet spirit had taken flight."[41]

After the deaths of Catherine in 1896 and Warren in 1898, the home would be lived in by Annie Delano Hitch and her husband, Fred Hitch.

Top: Algonac after a devastating fire gutted the house, 1916. *Franklin D. Roosevelt Library and Museum.*

Bottom: Algonac is brought back to life in a modern way. *Franklin D. Roosevelt Library and Museum.*

The house was used as the central hub for Delano family gatherings, including wedding parties and anniversaries. Various members of the family would use the home as a place to spend the night on their travels or just stop in and spend the weekend for old times' sake. On a cold Sunday afternoon in March 1916, a fire broke out in the attic of the home and raged for quite some time before it was discovered. Neighbors from the surrounding area came to the rescue of many of the belongings in the home, but Annie "sat on the lawn, wrapped in her fur coat, to watch her beloved home burn down."[42]

Warren III determined that the house should be rebuilt using as much of the original homestead as possible. Although many of the walls were still standing, they were not stable enough to be used in reconstruction, and it was determined that only portions of the foundation could be used in the construction of a new home. The architectural firm of Delano and Aldrich worked with some difficulty to design a modern home along the original footprint of the old house. Frederic Delano mentioned in his story in 1931 that "the result is a house which in many details is far more practical and comfortable than the old house."[43] The home was sold out of the family by the mid-twentieth century, and the estate itself has since been turned into separate small lots with modern houses. The grand old house stands alone on top of the hill with a few old tall trees to give it cover.

7

Mount Hope and Rosedale

In 1944, when FDR agreed to run for a fourth term as president, his letter of acceptance to the Democratic Party made it clear that this would be his final campaign. After years of service, he was eager to return to private life, saying, "All that is within me cries out to go back to my home on the Hudson River." Though there were many places along the Hudson where he had spent time that meant something to him, his heart belonged to Hyde Park. He considered himself more than just a politician in this town. He was a farmer, a neighbor, a concerned citizen and a friend. He served on the vestry at his spiritual home, St. James Church. He had been a volunteer firefighter at the local fire department. He looked on with admiration as his beloved mother gave money for the construction of the town's public library, which would be named after his father. He even agreed to serve as the town's first appointed historian. He would leave his mark on the town through a series of buildings, including a post office, school buildings and, of course, his presidential library. The little farming village along the Hudson just north of the city of Poughkeepsie is truly where the story of the Hyde Park Roosevelts began, and more to the point, it is where FDR's story began.

The first Roosevelt to make a home in the area of Hyde Park was FDR's great-grandfather James Roosevelt. He was the son of Isaac the Patriot and had spent the better part of his time in New York City. But like most city dwellers, the idea of a home in the country was the ultimate symbol of success. In 1818, James signed an agreement with Arthur Smith to sell him 270 acres in the town of Poughkeepsie in exchange for some of his properties

The Roosevelts at the town hall in Hyde Park, Election Day 1932. *Franklin D. Roosevelt Library and Museum.*

on Bleecker Street and Pearl Street in New York, as well as "three thousand four hundred dollars in cash" for a total value of $25,000.[44]

Mount Hope was built on the border of Hyde Park and Poughkeepsie on a hill overlooking the river, as with many of the country estates, between 1818 and 1820. The Roosevelts found themselves surrounded by grand families who had settled along the river's edge at least two centuries before them. Families like the Livingstons, Astors, Van Rensselaers and Schuylers had amassed large tracts of land and even larger fortunes that the Roosevelts would never come close to. James appears to have owned other buildings in nearby Poughkeepsie, as he had insured two brick buildings on Washington Street in 1842, one of which contained a silversmith shop, and a wood frame house on the corner of Main and Academy Streets.[45] Very little is known about the style and construction of Mount Hope, and sadly, no images exist of it. Many of the early Roosevelt papers and objects were in that home when it burned to the ground in September 1865.

Though James had built the house, it was his son Isaac, born in 1790, who would use it and make it into a true country farm. Though he had studied at the New York College of Physicians and Surgeons, Dr. Isaac Roosevelt hated medicine. He was afraid of the sight of blood, the wrath of God and any human being other than his immediate family members. In fact, Dr. Isaac was an oddity in the Roosevelt clan, as he was nothing like his charming and ambitious ancestors or decedents. Dr. Isaac decided to make a quiet life away from the city and its people and closer with nature. He moved into his father's Mount Hope estate, where his quiet pleasures included botanical experiments with his friend and future Hyde Park neighbor Dr. David Hosack and breeding cattle and horses.

In 1827, when Isaac was thirty-seven years old, he married his parents' New York neighbor, the eighteen-year-old Mary Rebecca Aspinwall. A year later, she gave birth at Mount Hope to their son, also named James, who would later become the father of the future president. After the birth of their son, Isaac and Mary decided that it was time to have a home of their own. They purchased land across from Mount Hope on the Albany Post Road and, in 1832, built a Federal-style home that they named Rosedale. The house sits high on the bluff about a mile inland from the river and was later modified by Isaac's second son, John Aspinwall Roosevelt. Later in the 1860s, John gave the house a more Italianate feel and added a servants' cottage and boathouse closer to the river, where he stored his prize-winning ice yacht.

By 1851, Isaac's first son, James Roosevelt, was finishing his studies at Harvard and deciding whether to have a career in law or in business; he would eventually decide on business. James was a quiet but ambitious man who hoped to acquire great wealth but never would. He had inherited money and Mount Hope from his grandfather, and in 1852, he was elected to the board of directors of the Consolidated Coal Company in Maryland. He also found himself in the railroad business serving as the general manager of the Cumberland and Pennsylvania lines. But this was nothing compared to some of the grand families like the Vanderbilts and Astors.

James married Rebecca Brien Howland in April 1853. Together, they would make Mount Hope a home of their own. It was here that James would teach their son, also named James, born in 1854, how to hunt and ride. One could only imagine how wonderful it would be to grow up on a lovely and secluded estate nestled in the hills above the mighty Hudson. Their young son, whom they nicknamed Rosy, had his every need met with a tutor, nurse,

The home of John A. Roosevelt, Rosedale, in 1889. *Franklin D. Roosevelt Library and Museum.*

dancing master and maid. The concerns of the rest of the world were far from sight at Mount Hope, and even when the country entered into the grips of a bloody Civil War by the 1860s, it appears that the Roosevelts played almost no part. In 1863, Dr. Isaac died, which left James with a considerable fortune, and his younger brother, John, inherited the Rosedale estate, where their mother was still living.

After the war, the family was eager to travel and sailed for Europe like so many other society families of New York. They enjoyed lavish hotels and restaurants wherever they went and dined with friends and distant relatives who were likeminded in their cultural pursuits. On September 17, 1865, news came from John in New York that Mount Hope had been burned to the ground. It was a total loss. The Roosevelts had let the house to William Griswold with the belief that the house would be safer if someone was living there while they were away. James felt that the fire was intentionally set by one of the Griswolds' servants, who didn't like the idea of spending time in the countryside and away from city life. Though this theory was never proven, it must have been told by James enough because FDR remembered it later in life. Sadly, much of the early history of the family went up in flames with that fire.

When they returned from their trip, James and Rebecca sold the property to "The People of the State of New York" on February 15, 1867, for the sum of $45,000.[46] Over the next several decades, the property that had been the Roosevelts' first home along the Hudson was transformed into a massive asylum known as the Hudson River State Hospital. When it opened in the 1870s, James agreed to serve as a lay adviser, which involved walking the wards and writing down his thoughts about living conditions and the care of patients. As he encountered numerous patients with various levels of mental illness along the way, it's interesting to ponder what his feelings might have been about his long-lost family home.

Grace and Ellen Roosevelt by Vail Brothers Studios, Poughkeepsie. *From the Local History Collections, Poughkeepsie Public Library District.*

John, who had inherited the Rosedale estate, married Ellen Murray Crosby, and they had two daughters, Grace and Ellen. Both girls would become champion tennis players not long after John decided to install a turf tennis court on the property at Rosedale in 1879. The girls used the court regularly to practice their new passion, and the self-taught duo did well in doubles. Ellen won the 1890 U.S. Open, playing Bertha Townsend in the finals.[47] After they ended their successful tennis careers at the close of the 1892 season, Grace married Appleton Clark in 1895 and moved to Staten Island. Ellen would inherit Rosedale when her father passed away in 1909. When Grace's husband died in 1930, she returned to Rosedale to live with her sister until her death in 1945. Ellen died in 1954, and the house was sold out of the family. It is in private hands today, surrounded by modern development.

8

SPRINGWOOD

After the devastation of the fire at Mount Hope, James Roosevelt wanted to find a suitable home for his wife, Rebecca, and young son, Rosy, but he had no intention of leaving his beloved Hudson River. Two suitable options came up for sale at about this time. The first was much farther north of Hyde Park, where you start to head into lands owned by prominent families like the Astors and what had once been the lords of Livingston Manor. James Roosevelt found himself quite tempted to purchase part of the Astor estate that became available in the 1860s. However, the price was simply not to his liking. The Astor family had made a fortune in real estate, so the asking price of $50,000 was out of the modest James's comfort zone.

However, just up the road from the ruins of his home was the house and farm of Josiah Wheeler. The property included 110 acres of farm and riverfront property, a lovely house with gardens and a horse track at the front of the property near the Albany Post Road, where James could exercise his trotting horses—all for $10,000 less than the Astor property. With the money that James had made from selling his land at Mount Hope to New York State for construction of the asylum, James decided to take the deal. The Roosevelts moved into their new home in 1867 and called it Springwood.

This property, known as Brierstone, was originally settled in 1790 by the "Widow Everson," as the historic structure report reads. Then, by 1827, Ephraim Holbrook and his wife, Nancy, had purchased the estate and built a square, two-story Federal-style home with gardens that were considered some of the loveliest around. The foundation of that house is still part of the

Springwood, view of the west side from the lower orchards. *Franklin D. Roosevelt Library and Museum.*

South side of Springwood with James Roosevelt sitting on the porch, October 1900. *Franklin D. Roosevelt Library and Museum.*

Roosevelt home today. Later, in the 1850s, Josiah and Mary Wheeler made major alterations to the house, including a three-story tower in the south end, bracketed cornices and a covered porch to give the house a more Italianate feel. The house stands close to the edge of a steep hill with sweeping views looking south down the river toward Poughkeepsie. The Wheelers had also built a Gothic Revival cottage for their gardener north of the house and flower gardens at about the same time.

There were very few alterations to the house during the years when James and Rebecca occupied it, as the estate appeared to have been to their liking from the start. James did add land to his farm when he purchased the land from neighboring properties belonging to the Boreel family. The Roosevelt farm fit the standards of "country place" ideals, which included large tracts of land that went along the river and ran inland a mile or so east, meticulously kept gardens, greenhouses, boathouses and stables, all with easy access to a train station so one could return to the city for business. James was fortunate enough to have stock in the railroads, so he decided to build a small siding along the railroad track at the bottom of his property along the river, so he did not have to head to Hyde Park station.

In 1876, James suffered the loss of his first wife, Rebecca, when she lost her battle with heart failure at the young age of forty-five. He buried her at St. James Church and mourned her loss for a few years. During that time, he gave his first son, Rosy, part of the Boreel property, which included a red clapboard house built in the 1830s, simply known as the Red House. Rosy had the good fortune of marrying Helen Astor in 1878, and with her came some of the famous Astor money. This new wealth certainly came in handy, as Rosy did not care much for employment but instead preferred to spend his time with his horses and coaches. That year, the couple moved into the Red House, which was just next door to his father, James. The Red House did not see much in the way of changes until the mid-twentieth century, when it was painted white and used as a law office. It now belongs to the National Park Service and is used as a private residence. It has been repainted and returned to its original color of dark red.

James Sr. lived only a few years alone in his home at Springwood before he fell in love again at the age of fifty-two. James had been invited to attend a party with some of his Oyster Bay cousins in New York City, when he met the young, beautiful and wealthy Sara Delano. She was twenty-six and the daughter of James's contemporary Warren Delano, whose home was just south in Newburgh. The couple were married in 1880 in a small ceremony at the Delano home, Algonac, where Sara had been born and spent many happy years. By the time she moved into the old house at Hyde Park, it clearly had the mark of James's first wife, and it was a little out of date, but Sara, perhaps out of respect for Rebecca, kept it that way until after her husband's death.

In this home, on January 30, 1882, Sara gave birth to her one and only child, Franklin Delano Roosevelt. The room where FDR first came into this world is located on the second floor of the south tower. Today, it is known as the Birth Room and still contains the original furnishings from the day of FDR's birth.

In the late nineteenth century, life at Springwood was ideal for the young Franklin Delano Roosevelt and his parents. The house and gardens were only enhanced by the natural beauty of the valley around them. The flowing streams in the area known as Kills brought fresh water into the river. Just beyond the deep river, the Shungunks and the Catskills could be seen to the west. The large variety of wildlife, particularly birds, satisfied FDR's curiosity for birding, and by his early teenage years, he had collected several hundred species, which his mother proudly displaced in the foyer of the house.

Inside the "Snuggery" before it was made smaller by the 1915 alterations. *Franklin D. Roosevelt Library and Museum.*

A young FDR with Sara and James Roosevelt on the south lawn of Springwood, 1891. *Franklin D. Roosevelt Library and Museum.*

The river is where FDR mastered his sailing, both in the summer with one of the family's sailboats and in the winter when the river froze over and the family would take to their ice yacht. FDR learned everything about sailing on the Hudson, which would benefit him in his later years as assistant secretary of the navy. The barns and stables were the pride of Mr. James, as he was lovingly referred to, since this is where he focused on his beloved trotters. James took great pride in his favorite horse, Gloster, who broke records for trotting in the 1870s. He kept the horses in a lovely coach house designed by Frederick Clarke Withers in 1886—the same man who had designed the state hospital that now stood where Mount Hope once was.

There were several other large and beautiful estates nearby, including Bellefield, owned by the Newbolds; Crumwold, owned by the Butlers and later the Rogerses; and Hyde Park, which at the time of FDR's birth was still in the hands of the Langdon family. Many of the neighbors in Hyde Park were close with one another. FDR spent time with the children of the Newbold and Rogers families and was even sent off for tutoring at Crumwold from time to time. All of these families also attended St. James Church, and FDR would consider all of them important friends in the course of his life.

James purchased a few additional parcels of land from several neighboring families, including the Brackens and Kirchners, bringing the total estate up to 623 acres.[48] He still left the house almost the same as when he purchased it, with the exception of a smoking room that was added off of the dining room and a bedroom above that on the second floor, though Eleanor Roosevelt proclaimed that nobody in the family ever liked using either space.[49] By the 1890s, most of their neighbors began to modernize and improve their houses with the latest fashions in architecture. The Rogerses had torn down the old Butler mansion, and their new home, Crumwold, was designed by Richard Morris Hunt in the Châteauesque style. The Langdon house was purchased by Frederick and Louise Vanderbilt, who hired the famous firm of McKim, Mead and White to build a larger and more modern version of the house they purchased. The firm also built two other homes in the area for the Vanderbilts in the Colonial Revival style—one of brick and the other in stone. Hyde Park kept McKim, Mead and White busy, as they also improved the home of the Mills family farther up in the village of Staatsburg and expanded Bellefield for the Newbold family, while landscape architect Beatrix Ferrand put in a lavish walled garden. All of these advancements occurred within a few miles of the Roosevelts, who continued to live in their old and outdated home.

James Roosevelt, who had suffered from various heart issues and strokes, died in 1900. In his will, he made sure to leave the house and property in the hands of his trusted wife, Sara, for the remainder of her life. Sara took to this new responsibility with vigor and endeavored to learn every aspect of estate management. However, both mother and son would share in the improvements of the Springwood estate, and as a team, they would expand the house for the next generation of Roosevelts.

After the death of his father, FDR continued his studies at Harvard. Sara detested the idea of being alone in Springwood and decided to rent a place in Cambridge so that she could be closer to her son. She would continue to oversee projects back home; for example, in 1903, she wanted the upstairs bedrooms painted and papered while she was away in Boston.[50] When FDR came home to Hyde Park during breaks in schoolwork, both mother and son dabbled in small alterations to their home. In 1904, the exterior of the house was repainted by John Clay, and Sara was very happy with the job, based on her diary entry that she underlined. The house was painted a dark olive green with a red trim.[51]

During this time, FDR was spending more time with his distant cousin Eleanor Roosevelt, who he had run into while on a train heading home to Hyde Park. As previously stated, Eleanor was born in New York City, but she had spent much of her childhood just north of where FDR had spent his. The cousins had bumped into one another at family gatherings, and they had even spent time together at Springwood when they were toddlers, so Eleanor had a distant memory of the place. After Eleanor and Franklin's wedding on St. Patrick's Day in 1905, the first part of their honeymoon was spent alone at Springwood before heading overseas.

By 1906, Eleanor and Franklin had the first of five children, Anna, who was born in New York City. She was followed by James the next year. By 1908, a new addition to the house was the installation of electricity, which Sara emphasized her pleasure with by mentioning it twice and underlining it in her diary: "Electric light is turned on, Electric light is turned on."[52] A son named Franklin Jr. was born in 1909 but died from heart failure in a few months. The infant was buried at St. James Church next to James and his first wife, Rebecca. After his death, Eleanor discovered she was with child again, and she gave birth to Elliott in 1910, also in New York City. In 1914, while the family was on vacation at their summer home on Campobello Island just off the coast of Maine, Eleanor had another son. They also named him Franklin Jr., as it was the custom to keep that name alive. While all of these children added to the family, Franklin and his mother decided to work on additions to their now crowded home.

Beginning in 1915, but perhaps even earlier, plans were being considered for the alterations and additions to Springwood. Based on a letter between Sara and her son, who was now serving as assistant secretary of the navy, she was hoping that Charles Platt, the architect she had hired to design their townhouse, would be able to take on this project as well. However, he was too busy with other endeavors in and around the city. Instead, Sara found an architect named Frances Hoppin to work on the house. Another letter from Sara to her son suggests that FDR had made some drawings of what he was thinking the house should be, and she then handed the drawings off to Hoppin.[53] Based on letters between FDR, his mother and Hoppin, the project was a team effort, with each one putting in their thoughts as to how things should be done, clearly with expenses in mind. FDR had hired his friend Elliott Brown to do the construction.[54] The main block of the original house remained intact, with the south parlor on the first floor, also known as the "Snuggery," and the east room on the second floor directly above it, now known as the Birth Room, being cut in half to allow access to a southern wing built with fieldstone. The clapboard exterior to the original house was removed and stucco was applied.

In September 1915, one of the workmen cut a beam in the center of the house, which caused the middle of the second floor to sink, as Sara told her son in a letter. She also thought that she would have to have the hall and some of the bedrooms plastered all over again due to the sinking.[55] By

Construction on the northeast end of Springwood, showing piles of local fieldstone, 1915. *Franklin D. Roosevelt Library and Museum.*

October 1915, the layout of the library was coming along, and FDR was very pleased that Hoppin was able to work in plenty of shelves for his growing book collection, as well as larger spaces for his model ships.[56] Based on Sara's personal checkbooks, it appears that she paid for the entire project, well over $45,000 between contractors and architect fees. By the early spring of 1916, the house was just about complete and looked more like the mansions that were close by than it had before. The stone and stucco Colonial Revival style had replaced the clapboard and Italianate. The south side tower that once stood tall above the rest of the house now blended in with a third floor. Some of the cornices on the river side and the servants' wing of the house were left in place. Today, they remain as evidence of the older style of home.

The house now had plenty of space to handle the Roosevelt family's size, which would expand once again at the completion of the home improvements, when on March 13, they welcomed their final child, John. Eleanor noted in her autobiography that she felt that she was always either pregnant or giving birth for ten years straight, but luckily, she had many servants and her mother-in-law to help with the day-to-day work of

Progress on the construction work of Springwood with two of the Roosevelt children standing on the new porch. *Franklin D. Roosevelt Library and Museum.*

managing five young children. Besides the alterations to the house, FDR also included an additional safety feature of fireproofing the new wings. He included metal doors that would close if a fire broke out, thus protecting the new wings. Throughout the house, one will also notice the old-fashioned fire extinguisher bulbs that were once filled with carbon tetrachloride.

Beginning in 1911, FDR started buying land from his neighbors around Hyde Park. First, he purchased the Bennett farm, which was about 194 acres and located to the east of his father's land heading across Violet Avenue.[57] This is where he would begin working on his forestry projects, and between 1912 and 1916, he purchased forty-two thousand trees to plant, including white pine, Scotch pine and Norway spruce.[58] Even during the 1920s, as he was recovering from polio and from losing his first election in his run for vice president, FDR began making plans to purchase another piece of property, the Tompkins Farm. Mrs. Sarah Tompkins had inherited about 192 acres and an eighteenth-century farmhouse at the intersection of Creek Road and Violet Avenue, and FDR purchased it from her in 1925 for $7,000.[59]

FDR continued to take great interest in his tree plantation at Hyde Park, even during the Great Depression. William Plog, the superintendent of the family's estate at Hyde Park, sent FDR regular updates on planting and work. In 1935, Mr. Plog sent the president a list of men who worked on over one thousand tulip poplars as well as white pines. Each man put in about four days of work at a wage of three dollars a day.[60] FDR kept up

Above: Springwood during the years of FDR's presidency. Notice the special railing and the presidential flag. *Franklin D. Roosevelt Library and Museum.*

Left: FDR and his mother, Sara, on the porch at Springwood during the 1920 presidential campaign. *Franklin D. Roosevelt Library and Museum.*

with studies and suggestions on forestry sent to him by Professor Nelson Brown from the State Forestry College in Syracuse. Not only did FDR take his own forests very seriously, but he also thought it was a good idea for all communities to do so. He wrote to Brown in 1939, saying, "I believe more of our communities could profit economically, socially, and spiritually by ownership and operation of their own forests close at home."[61] Besides his own estate, millions of trees would be planted across the country under his administration in the hopes of preventing future dust bowls.

His tree farm was, of course, not without its issues, as Eleanor wrote about in her column "My husband, after a tour of inspection of his young Christmas trees, planted this spring, found the percentage of loss appalling. They had tried to water them, but with a rather primitive watering cart which takes about a week to water the area."[62]

By the 1940s, Brown had informed FDR that his Christmas tree operation was doing quite well, and his profits were growing with each year. By 1943, he had made about $2,750 just on Christmas trees.[63] These were good business for the Roosevelts, and FDR took pride in his trees being sent to various world leaders during the war. Prime Minister Winston Churchill of England and Princess Martha of Norway both received a tree. However, he also enjoyed sending them to his relatives nearby. Just days after Pearl Harbor, he wrote to Mr. Plog asking him to get two eight-foot trees to send to his cousins Daisy Suckley and Laura Delano in Rhinebeck.[64] After FDR's death, Eleanor and her son Elliott continued the business of selling trees for a short time. In 1948, she wrote in My Day about a trip she made with her son to the city, where on 124th Street, there was a lot where their trees were for sale.[65]

Sara had continued to oversee the farm just as her husband had done before. James Roosevelt had established what he called the Home Farm on the east side of Post Road and maintained cows, horses, pigs and chickens. There was a large vegetable garden that took care of the needs of the estate just north of the main house. Sara did not stray far from the methods that James had used, including keeping up the herd of cows. FDR never really saw the need for a large herd, as he mentioned in a letter to his friend James Townsend from Poughkeepsie, who sometimes wrote to him about his mother's farm: "I really think that four cows are ample for the milk needed except, of course, on the very rare weekends when I am at home with a big party or Mrs. Roosevelt has a lot of people at the cottage." He went on to say that it would be "more economical for her to buy milk in Poughkeepsie at such times."[66]

Aerial view of the Roosevelt estate before the presidential library was added, 1932. *Franklin D. Roosevelt Library and Museum.*

The Roosevelt estate was home to more than just the president and his family. FDR was a landlord to several tenants, including those who worked for him, like Moses Smith, Peter Rohan and William Plog. Though, arguably, he was not the best when it came to getting things fixed in a timely manner. Mrs. Moses Smith wrote to the president on October 24, 1938, to inform him of a promise he had made long before he was president or even governor. She reminded him that he, Eleanor, Marian Dickerman and Nancy Cook had visited them at their home on Violet Avenue, which once stood directly across Violet Avenue from the entrance to Eleanor's Val-Kill cottage. She told him that during the visit "you noticed the dining room and kitchen floors and told me that you would give me new flooring." Almost ten years had passed, and the floors had started to sag even worse than before. Mrs. Smith said that she had tried to convince her husband to nudge the president, but "he said that you were too busy; now I feel that it is my duty to tell you the condition of the house as it is an old one and well worth saving."[67] FDR finally got around to hiring Jim Van Wagner of Hyde Park to do all of the work needed on the Smith farmhouse in

Above: Inside the south living room and library of Springwood. *Franklin D. Roosevelt Library and Museum.*

Right: Dining room showing a portrait of Franklin Hughes Delano. *Franklin D. Roosevelt Library and Museum.*

December. It cost $343, which FDR claimed was $43 more than what he wanted to spend.

When the president visited his mother's house, he never went alone. The house was surprisingly small for the sort of weekend visits that came with being the mother of the president, and though Sara was a gracious host, she was not always thrilled with some of FDR's guests. Louis Howe was a regular who bothered all of her senses, from the smoking to the foul language and generally pushing her son to do things that she considered dangerous for his well-being. However, she seemed to glow when King George and Queen Elizabeth of England came for the weekend in 1939. She was pleased even if she had to endure the presence of the White House servants instead of her own, which was the wish of the president and first lady. The assignment of rooms could be tricky when it came to royalty, as queens and other such women of high rank generally brought with them a lady-in-waiting. After Sara's death, the placement of visitors in the house became the responsibility of the president's secretary, Gracy Tully, as we see in a memo from July 1942, where she placed the Queen of the Netherlands in the Pink Room, her lady-in-waiting in the little green room next door and Princess Juliana in the Chintz Room. The queen and her daughter would have shared the bathroom in the middle.[68]

During World War II, the president entertained Prime Minister Winston Churchill at Springwood several times, but by that point, the house was in the process of becoming something quite different from the home it once was. On September 7, 1941, FDR sat at his mother's bedside, which was in the room at the end of the south hall of the second floor. She had given birth to her only son in this bed, and this is where she passed away at the age of eighty-six. An era had come to a close with one of the last of New York's great dowagers ending her reign at Hyde Park. A few days later, a simple service took place in the library of the home, with the Reverend Frank Wilson reading excerpts from the book of common prayer.[69] FDR buried his mother beside his father and several other relatives at the cemetery at St. James Church. The president had lost one of the most important and influential figures in his world just before his biggest test yet: the entry into World War II.

Before his mother's passing, FDR had convinced her and the rest of the family that the "big house" should be preserved for history's sake. Part of his reasoning was because he had decided that he would build a presidential library that would house his personal collections and presidential papers for historians to study his work and his family's history. He wanted this building to be near home and drew up plans for it to be placed in his mother's front

View of the Dresden room, named for the Dresden porcelain on display. *Franklin D. Roosevelt Library and Museum.*

yard. By the 1930s, his personal collections had expanded well beyond the bounds of his modest home. He had over fifteen thousand books; hundreds of model ships, naval prints and political cartoons; and well over a million stamps.[70] That didn't include the countless papers he had accumulated over the course of his private and political life. After successfully convincing his mother, he gave a sixteen-acre parcel of land, which sits just east of the rose garden, to the government for the first presidential library.

The library was constructed over the course of a few years, starting with a small sketch that FDR made in 1937. To build the library, he used private funds of about $376,000 and brought in the help of his architectural friend Henry Toombs, though the project eventually went to architect Louis A. Simon to complete. Ground was broken in September 1939, which allowed FDR to place a cornerstone on November 10. FDR kept a close eye on the work over the next year. He wanted all of the materials to be locally sourced, and he wanted it to resemble, like many of the other buildings he had a hand in, the Dutch Colonial style that he loved.[71] The library was then handed over to the government to be maintained by the National Archives and was formally dedicated on June 30, 1941. FDR used the library during his presidency, even broadcasting a few of his famous fireside chats live from his little office. In 1972, two new wings were added in honor of Eleanor Roosevelt, based on the plans that FDR had already considered much earlier.

At about the same time that the work was beginning on his library, FDR was finishing the final details for his plan to give his family's home to the government. On July 18, 1939, a joint resolution was made to allow for the acceptance of the Roosevelt home to become a national park.[72] By 1940, the National Park Service had photographed the entire home to have a

FDR sitting in his new presidential library office, 1942. *Franklin D. Roosevelt Library and Museum.*

Eleanor Roosevelt and President Truman at the dedication of the Home of FDR National Historic Site, 1946. *Franklin D. Roosevelt Library and Museum.*

proper record of the furnished interior for later interpretive use. FDR made sure to allow for his family to continue to have use of the home if they so desired. However, after his death on April 12, 1945, it did not take long for the family to agree that the home should be turned over to the government almost immediately. When the family officially vacated the home around November 1945, they left it almost completely intact, with the exception of a few mementos to remember their father. The National Park Service took the next several months to restore the home and prepare it for the thousands of tourists that they knew would come.

On April 12, 1946, a year after the president's death, the Home of FDR National Historic Site opened its doors to visitors for the first time. President Truman, Eleanor Roosevelt, members of the United Nations and even his dog, Fala, stood on the front porch of the home, where speeches of tribute were given to the longest-serving president.[73] Today, his home is still the only national park that is the birthplace, residence and burial site of a U.S. president.

Some of the first visitors take a peek inside FDR's bedroom. Notice his wheelchair on display. Most Americans had never seen it up close before. *Franklin D. Roosevelt Library and Museum.*

In its first years open to the public, the admission fee was fifty cents, and by 1947, over half a million people had walked through the home, pushing the National Park Service to install new carpeting and better boundaries.[74] Sadly, on January 23, 1982, almost one hundred years after FDR's birth, a fire broke out in the attic of the house and quickly spread across the roof. The fire, which proved to be due to an electrical issue, caused massive amounts of smoke and water damage and destroyed most of the original wallpaper. Curators ran through the house removing paintings and covering furnishings as smoke billowed and firemen made their way past with hoses.[75] It took many years of cleaning and restoration work before the house was finally ready for visitors again.

In January 2020, the National Park Service was preparing for another major restoration project. The contents of the home were moved out and contractors were brought in for a major cleanup of the interior and exterior of the home, as well as a rehabilitation of the home's heating and cooling systems. This project was estimated to take the better part of the year, so

The view from FDR's bedroom window shows the Hudson and the bridges near Poughkeepsie in the distance. *Franklin D. Roosevelt Library and Museum.*

the Roosevelt home shut down during this process to allow the restoration team to take on the project without visitors being underfoot. When it is complete, the home will have a new HVAC system, new fire and intrusion systems and fresh paint and plaster, just to name a few improvements.[76] The house is in need of this sort of treatment, as it has been "loved to death" over the years, like so many national treasures. FDR would be glad to see the love that his home has received, both in the appreciation from visitors and in the care given by National Park Service staff. And he would be happy to know that so many people continue to cherish Springwood, just as he once did.

St. James Church

J ames and Sara baptized their son at the St. James Chapel about a mile and a half up the road from Springwood at the center of town. Sara had converted to her husband's Episcopal faith when they married, and both contributed to the well-being of St. James's parish. In the winter, they went to the small chapel on East Market Street, as it was easier to heat than the larger church that was located farther north on the Albany Post Road. For many of those of the Christian faith, a church can certainly be seen as a home for the spirit or a temporary residence for the religious. In other words, the building itself can be a place where you feel at home with your chosen deity and members of your spiritual family. For the Roosevelt family, that spiritual home was St. James Episcopal Church, with a history that goes back to the very beginnings of the town of Hyde Park.

St. James was founded by some of the earliest and most prominent settlers of the Hyde Park area at the turn of the nineteenth century. The land where the main church stands once belonged to the Bard family, and in the early 1800s, Dr. Samuel Bard donated land where his father, Dr. John Bard, was buried for the creation of a church and graveyard. Dr. Samuel Bard was perhaps the first famous person to call the area of Hyde Park his home. Bard had been a surgeon like his father and even served as the physician to George Washington. Bard is perhaps most famous for helping to build a medical school at King's College, now Columbia University. Bard, along with some other big names in the area, including Governor Morgan Lewis, James Duane Livingston, Nathaniel Pendleton and Tobias Stoutenburgh,

View from the choir loft at St. James Episcopal Church, 2020. *Photo taken by the author.*

raised $2,576.75, plus an extra contribution of $125.00, for the building of the church.[77] On Easter Sunday 1812, a meeting of the congregation was held in which they decided that the name of the church would be St. James Church of Hyde Park.

In the early days of the church, it was small, measuring only about thirty by fifty feet.[78] It was also small with regard to parishioners, but more and more people were being confirmed into the church with each passing year. Another interesting part of the church's humble beginning was that its first sexton was enslaved during his first several years of caring for the buildings and grounds. Richard Jenkins was born into slavery sometime around 1783, when New York was still a long way away from ending the evil business. He had been enslaved by Bard, and it appears that he began laboring at the church around 1817. Since the St. James history shows that he served as the sexton for forty years and he died in 1857, that means he was still enslaved when he began the work, probably at the order of his enslaver, who built the church to begin with. By 1822, his name appears in the treasury report as a paid employee, which means that he must have been given his freedom when Bard died in 1821.[79]

The Reverend Samuel Roosevelt Johnson, who was elected to serve the church in 1824, decided to build a schoolhouse in the village of Hyde Park, just under a mile south of the church.[80] It is in the Greek Revival style, with Doric columns facing toward the north on East Market Street. The school served several members of the parish, and in 1834, Reverend Johnson gave the building to the church for its continued use. It later became a small library and reading room used by the villagers. Later, in 1856, a small Gothic-style chapel was added to the school, and it was small enough to be heated, unlike the main church, which would not have heat until the mid-twentieth century.[81] In the winter, this chapel became the main place for services, hence FDR's baptism there in the winter of 1882.

The church had several different rectories over the course of its existence, including one just north of the church known as the Red House, which was built by the Bard family. FDR had used a drawing of the Red House for his inspiration for the Hyde Park Post Office. Though the Bard home had been built using clapboard instead of stone, FDR could not break away from his passion for stone buildings.[82] The Hyde Park Post Office was built in 1941, and FDR dedicated it himself. That rectory was later replaced by a separate house in the center of the village of Hyde Park. This house, which still sits on Park Place, is an old Greek Revival building that was built in 1848 by the Livingston family. Archibald Rogers and Elbridge T. Gerry purchased the house in 1895 to be used as a rectory, and the old Bard house was torn down. The church continued to use this rectory on Park Place until 1957, when the current rectory, which stands just north of the church today, was built. The house at Park Place would turn into apartments, and their most famous resident was most certainly Eleanor Roosevelt's longtime friend and confidant Lorena Hickok. She moved into a downstairs apartment in the late 1950s.[83] Hickok was said to have been well liked by all of the young boys in the neighborhood, who brought her much-needed comfort after Eleanor Roosevelt passed away. She would stand in the front yard in a man's shirt and baggy pants with a cigarette hanging from her lips, handing out cookies to the boys who walked by.[84]

FDR's father served the church first on the vestry beginning in 1858, when he was thirty years old and was married to his first wife, Rebecca. By the end of his life, he had served as the senior warden, using his sense of business to better the church's financial position. When he died in 1900, a stained-glass window was ordered by Sara and installed in his honor.[85] James's son from his first marriage, Rosy, also served the church for many years, and a plaque in his honor still rests on the south wall of the church.

St. James Chapel and reading room on East Market Street. *From the collection of the Hyde Park Free Library.*

St. James Rectory on Park Place, which later became apartments. *From the collection of the Hyde Park Free Library.*

When FDR's turn to serve on the vestry came, he happily accepted, beginning in 1906. By 1929, even while serving as governor of New York, FDR was part of a major fundraising effort, along with fellow warden and neighbor Edmund P. Rogers, to fix the church's deficit. Rogers and FDR had to squeeze $1,500 out of the villagers, which would then be matched by fellow Episcopalian and neighbor Frederick Vanderbilt.[86] FDR asked his mother; the wife of his half-brother, Rosy; and his next-door neighbors, the Newbold family, to chip in. They managed to pull it off. He would continue to play a major role in church decisions through the rest of his life. FDR's son James once referred to his father as a "frustrated clergyman," and we can hear tones similar to those of good clergy in his speeches where he asks for God's assistance.

In his life, FDR turned to a few important clergymen for spiritual guidance, including his former headmaster at Groton, Reverend Endicott Peabody, and Reverend Frank Wilson, who served St. James and the town of Hyde Park for over a decade. In the correspondence between FDR and Reverend Wilson, we see him asking for guidance during the Great Depression, when the country was at its worst. On September 23, 1935, FDR wrote to Wilson, saying, "Because of the grave responsibilities of my office I am turning to representative clergymen for counsel and advice—feeling confident that no group can give more accurate or unbiased views." When he could, FDR would bring leaders of the world to St. James, hoping that they would find similar spiritual peace that he found there. This included the King and Queen of England during their whirlwind visit in 1939. Years later, Secretary of the Treasury and Hudson Valley neighbor Henry Morgenthau, who had a farm just south of Hyde Park in Fishkill, told the rector of the church that he had attended more services at St. James Church with the Roosevelts than at his own synagogue alone.[87]

When FDR died in April 1945, his casket made its way up the river via train to Hyde Park, where it stopped at the private landing that his father had paid for years ago. From there, the casket was taken off the Pullman car and placed on a military truck that was capable of bringing the heavy copper casket up to the lower field just south of Springwood. From there, it was placed on a horse-drawn caisson for the final trek to the rose garden.[88] FDR had planned out exactly how he wanted his funeral and burial to go. He had buried his beloved mother in the graveyard at St. James only a few years before his own death. Though most of his family and many of his Hyde Park friends were buried at this hollow ground, FDR had already decided to be buried at home. He made these plans in December 1937, on a

Left: The Reverend Frank Wilson and FDR have a chat after service in 1936. *Franklin D. Roosevelt Library and Museum.*

Below: The graveside service in the rose garden at Springwood, April 15, 1945. *Franklin D. Roosevelt Library and Museum.*

little memorandum to his son James, which read, "A plain white monument, no carving or decoration."

The burial service took place in the garden at Springwood and was presided over by the Reverend Dr. W. George Anthony, who had taken over for Reverend Wilson when he left to serve in the war. After a few prayers, the West Point Cadets who lined up on the western end of the garden fired their salute. From there, the guests made their way up Albany Post Road to the church for the full service. NBC correspondents were there to report on the event, which began in the church with a reading from one of FDR's favorite parts of the New Testament, 1 Corinthians 13, followed by singing of some of his favorite hymns.[89] Meanwhile, outside the church, hundreds of neighbors and onlookers stood in silence during the course of the service. A few years later, a marble memorial was placed inside the church by Eleanor and the new rector, the Reverend Gordon Kidd, who took over the parish not long after FDR's funeral. This memorial was placed at the front of the church near the memorials dedicated to the founders of the church, the Bard family, and not far from his father's memorial window. Even before FDR's memorial was added, St. James was famous for its cluttered walls and was referred to as "the Westminster Abbey of this section of the state."[90]

The next time St. James would see crowds like those of FDR's funeral was in 1962, for Eleanor's funeral. The *New York Times* showcased several photos of the scene at the church for the private service and the burial service in the Roosevelt rose garden. The list of attendees was nothing short of remarkable, as every president who had served since FDR was in attendance, including Harry S. Truman, Dwight D. Eisenhower and John F. Kennedy, even though Eleanor had annoyed all of them with her insistence on civil rights legislation. Future president Lyndon B. Johnson was also present, no doubt recalling the time Eleanor had invited him to Hyde Park, the home of his hero, FDR. Two New York governors were present, Supreme Court justices, United Nations ambassadors and New Dealers from FDR's cabinet, Frances Perkins and James A. Farley, just to name a few.[91]

Unlike FDR's funeral, Eleanor's casket was first placed in the church for the full service, which included a eulogy, before slowly making its way down the Albany Post Road to the Roosevelt estate and rose garden burial.[92] All of the town of Hyde Park clustered around the sides of the road to see the funeral procession go by. They had all been so used to seeing Eleanor in her Fiat convertible driven by her gardener, Tubby Curran. The Reverend Gordon Kidd remarked at the gravesite, "The entire world becomes one family orphaned by her passing. Her deep concern for the welfare of all

The Reverend Gordon Kidd and Eleanor Roosevelt unveil a memorial to FDR inside St. James Church, 1948. *Franklin D. Roosevelt Library and Museum.*

peoples, her understanding of their problems, and her efforts in their behalf gained this most remarkable woman a permanent place in the hearts of all."[93]

Over the course of the next twenty-five years, all of the Roosevelt children would be laid to rest at the Roosevelt plot at St. James, with the exception of eldest son James, who died in 1991 and is buried in California, where he had served as a U.S. congressman.[94] There would not be another funeral quite so large as Franklin or Eleanor Roosevelt's.

The newspaper headlines on the morning of June 11, 1984, are still enough to break any churchgoer's heart. The first line of the *Poughkeepsie Journal* read, "A suspicious fire Sunday destroyed the interior of the 140-year-old Hyde Park church that served as the spiritual home of Franklin and Eleanor Roosevelt."[95] The fire, which was believed to be arson, broke out on the far west end of the church, near the front door and bell tower. The flames were so intense that the pipes from the organ and the church bells were melted beyond recognition. Slate from the roof fell on firemen who came from five different fire departments, all but one of the historic stained-glass windows were blown out and many of the famous memorials were charred beyond repair. It would take longer than a year to clean up the church enough to have services again. Over time, the stained-glass would be remade, though not all original designs were reproduced. Interestingly, the window dedicated to James Roosevelt was remade but with an incorrect death date, reading that he died in 1909 instead of 1900.

Today, the parish is still as active as ever. The chapel where FDR was baptized has been restored to its former glory with the help of parishioners John and Gloria Golden. Mr. Golden attended the church in FDR's day, and Mrs. Golden's father was the Reverend Gordon Kidd, who served the church for over twenty years, beginning in 1946. The church considers its place in history to be a tool in its ministry efforts for education. Looking back on the old school that was part of the chapel, today, the church operates a daycare in the parish hall. Every year, guided tours are offered through the historic graveyard, where actors re-create the lives of fascinating characters near the graves and mausoleums where they are laid to rest. Fireside Chats take place in the winter and early spring, where scholars give lectures on local and Roosevelt history. As long as there is a need, St. James Church will continue to serve Hyde Park, both spiritually and educationally.

Val-Kill, the Business and the Home

E leanor Roosevelt had lived in other people's homes for over half of her life. For her, it was usually hard to find peace and comfort in just about every household she had been in since she was a child. She would later admit that she always felt as if she were a guest in every place from her grandmother's home where she grew up to her mother-in-law's home where she raised a family. What made it even more challenging was her husband's political career, which meant that the family was often moving in and out of public servant housing that did not belong to them. That went on for half of her life, until she finally managed to build a place of her own.

The idea for Val-Kill cottage was not so much Eleanor's as it was FDR's, which was recalled years later by one of Eleanor's old friends. In the fall of 1924, FDR, Eleanor, her two friends Marion Dickerman and Nancy Cook and three of the Roosevelt children, John, Franklin Jr. and Anna, were enjoying a picnic by the stream known as the Fal-kill. *Kill* is the word for "stream" in the old Dutch language, which can be seen all over the Hudson Valley in local names. Marion told the story in a book that was published in 1974, titled *Invincible Summer*, that she had heard Eleanor complaining that the picnic they were enjoying would be the last for the year. The reason for this concern was that FDR's mother was closing Springwood, as was customary for that time of year, and the family would be heading to the city for the winter. FDR replied to her with the idea that the three women should have a place of their own right on the spot where they sat, since that land belonged to him and not his mother. He had purchased the land they were

Eleanor takes Fala for a walk on the grounds at Val-Kill, 1948. *Franklin D. Roosevelt Library and Museum.*

enjoying in 1911 from the Bennett family. In the 1920s, the land was being used mostly as a dairy and chicken farm, where FDR's tenant farmer, Moses Smith, lived and worked.[96] FDR mentioned to Nancy and Marian that it would be an excellent spot for them to build a country home, and he would give them life interest in the land with the understanding that the property would be returned to his estate after their deaths.[97]

The plan for the cottage may have even started before that famous picnic, as suggested by Kenneth Davis in *Invincible Summer*, as FDR had written a letter in August 1924 to his friend Elliott Brown that read, "My missus and some of her female political friends want to build a shack on a stream in the back woods."[98] FDR also had great interest in building a pool somewhere on the Roosevelt estate, and it was decided that it would be part of the Val-Kill project that was taking form. Lewis Howe, the Roosevelts' friend and political advisor, witnessed the three women and FDR sign the document that allowed them to use the property. The relationship between Eleanor, Marion and Nancy had started a few years before this agreement was signed.

Marion Dickerman looks over plans for the stone cottage, 1925. *From the Dickerman Collection, Roosevelt-Vanderbilt National Historic Site.*

Eleanor met Nancy in 1922 at a fundraising event for women Democrats, where Nancy was looking for someone with a big name to help her spread the word. The two of them hit it off right away. Nancy introduced Eleanor to her partner, Marion, and for almost a decade, the three women were nearly inseparable.

Both Nancy and Marion were well educated and came from New York families with Protestant backgrounds. Marion had attended Wellesley, while Nancy went to Syracuse University. Both had seen action overseas during the First World War; Marion served in the Red Cross, and Nancy used her woodworking skills to craft artificial limbs for wounded soldiers. And of course, both women were heavily involved in the fight for women's right to vote. Marion even came back from Europe after the war to discover that she had been nominated to run for the New York State Assembly—the first woman to have that honor. This new friendship was one of many that helped morph Eleanor into an independent woman. FDR found their friendship to be beneficial to him as well, since the more Democratic women he had on his side, the better his chances for office.

In early 1925, plans for what the cottage would look like started to emerge. One of Eleanor's political friends, Caroline O'Day, had a talented cousin, Henry Toombs, who had worked for the famous architectural firm of McKim, Mead and White. He designed plans for a Dutch Colonial cottage, which were then approved by Eleanor, Marion and Nancy. FDR played a major role in the architectural portion of the project, as he had always had an interest in early Dutch houses in the Hudson Valley. He

Progress is being made on the construction of the stone cottage, 1925. *From the Dickerman Collection, Roosevelt-Vanderbilt National Historic Site.*

added his thoughts to Toombs's plans when he noticed the Palladian-style windows that Toombs had drawn onto the house. Roosevelt's handwritten notes in pencil read, "Flat tops to windows! Please!" This shows us that he knew what he wanted, and more to the point, he knew what was accurate in early Dutch architecture.

Besides the desire to have a place of their own, Eleanor, Marion and Nancy, along with Caroline O'Day, considered the potential for economic growth, as their cottage idea was evolving with each passing day. During another picnic by the stream, the politically minded team of women considered the conditions of the locals around them. It had become clear that many young people were leaving the countryside and heading to the city to find more lucrative careers. The agricultural way of life in Dutchess County and other surrounding rural areas was not what it had been fifty years before. It was discussed that the Val-Kill cottage could be used as a site of a small cottage industry that could be an example for others across the country to follow. Nancy had wanted to get back into her previous career of teaching students the art of woodworking and furniture making, and she had mentioned the idea of teaching young men how to re-create early American furniture patterns.[99] The women believed that if the young people of the area could learn these skills, they would be more likely to stay on their farms and sell homemade furniture when times were hard.

The group of women seemed happy to take on any projects that came to mind, including a women's Democratic magazine. Even before the idea for the furniture factory, they joined together to purchase a bulletin from the New York Democratic Women's Division and turned it into a monthly magazine.[100] In it, Caroline O'Day hinted at the future of Val-Kill cottage and what it meant to them: "When politics is through with us we are retiring to this charming retreat that is now rearing its stone walls against the beautiful cedars of a Dutchess County hillside."[101] It is still unclear why O'Day would write this, as she does not appear to have had any finances put into the cottage. Instead, we see evidence of Eleanor, Marion and Nan sharing an account and putting equal amounts of cash into a savings for their cottage projects.[102]

Bids were coming in for the construction of the cottage, but FDR felt they were too high. The prices did not seem to bother Marion and Nancy, who simply wished to get the project underway. FDR and Henry Toombs, however, insisted on taking over the matter. "If you three girls will just go away and leave us alone," FDR proclaimed, "Henry and I will build the cottage." So, it was agreed that Eleanor, Marion and Nan would venture to the Roosevelt summer home in Campobello while FDR and Toombs hashed out deals with contractors. Construction began in the summer of 1925, with FDR saving the women almost $5,000 on the project, a fact that he took great joy in reminding them of from time to time.[103]

As work progressed on the house and the pool that FDR wanted, the friends were deciding how to furnish the home and what appliances were needed. It was agreed by both Eleanor and Marion that the majority of the furnishings should be the work of Nancy, who had been studying and sketching the patterns of early furniture located in the collections of the Metropolitan Museum of Art.[104] Originally, part of the small cottage was dedicated as a workshop for Nancy to create her furnishings. There would be a small kitchen, a living room with a big fireplace, a bedroom on the first floor and a large bedroom on the second floor, which could be used in a dormitory sort of fashion. On the second floor, Eleanor, Marion and Nan would spend many nights staying up discussing issues and politics like college girls.

On January 1, 1926, though it was not yet furnished, and the smell of fresh paint lingered, the first meal at Val-Kill was served. A celebration for the completion of their dream took place with the three friends, FDR, his mother and some family. They sat on kegs around a makeshift table and toasted to the success of a well-built home. Eleanor finally had a place that felt like home to her, though it was still a shared home. She had always resented the townhouse on East Sixty-Fifth Street since her mother-in-law still held the title, and she felt like a permanent guest at Springwood. The family's summer home in Canada, Campobello, did have its charms, and she and Franklin could say that it was really, truly theirs, but they only spent a small portion of each summer there.

Val-Kill, which FDR nicknamed the "Honeymoon Cottage," was something Eleanor could use at any point of the year, and she made it quite clear, especially to Sara, that it was a separate entity from Springwood, which the family began referring to as the "Big House." Sara never showed any outward feelings regarding the new designation; however, it is likely that she did not like the idea of Eleanor leaving the big mansion to live in a little shack by the stream. Though Sara did write to FDR in 1926, saying, "Eleanor is so happy over there that she looks well and plump, don't tell her so, it is very becoming."[105]

The main interest in the site was, of course, the outdoors, where they had first enjoyed their summer picnics. Val-Kill's outdoor aspects were just as important as the cottage itself—from the patios and the pool to the stream and the woods. Nature inspired them, and they enjoyed it to the fullest. Most of the photographs taken at Val-Kill are of outdoor activities like pool parties and picnics. FDR loved the pool and used it not just for his physical therapy but also to keep cool. In August 1933, the *New York Times* devoted an article to the fact that the president could no longer handle the heat at his desk in his mother's house, so he drove to Val-Kill for a swim.[106] It was Nancy's idea to build a beautiful outdoor fireplace, where FDR could cook his meat the way he liked it. The fireplace was built out of local fieldstone sometime around 1933. Nancy took the landscaping and the gardens quite seriously. She did most of the work herself, and she installed a vegetable and a flower garden as well as a sprinkler system.[107]

As the idea for the cottage industry morphed, they realized that a bigger building would be needed to take on their plan for making and selling furniture. Nancy had begun working on her projects inside the stone cottage. In fact, that was where she had made many of the furnishings the friends used inside the cottage. However, more room was needed if they truly wanted to bring in unemployed farmers and teach them the self-sustainable craft of furniture making. Nancy and Henry Toombs worked on the factory project together. Cook and FDR had already discussed the idea of a garage and living quarters to be built with a shop space for working, which would all be built rather cheaply.[108] So, unlike the Dutch Colonial home that inspired FDR to take part, he had very little to do with the work on the factory.

Construction for the factory began in 1926, with Eleanor paying for most of the construction and Marion and Nancy paying for the machinery and

Inside the completed stone cottage, showing off some of the pieces made in the furniture factory. *Roosevelt-Vanderbilt National Historic Site.*

FDR with friends and family at the pool at Val-Kill. *Roosevelt-Vanderbilt National Historic Site.*

Picnic near the stone grill at Val-Kill, 1927. *Roosevelt-Vanderbilt National Historic Site.*

supplies. The total cost ended up being around $11,470, and the industry was well underway by 1927.[109] Their first employee was Frank Landolfa, a skilled cabinetmaker from Italy, who didn't like the rural feeling of Hyde Park. Eleanor saw in him a real talent, and she did everything she could think of to keep him happy and employed at Val-Kill, including helping him buy a car, sending him to night class to improve his English speaking skills and taking care of his room and board.[110] Later additions would be added to the building between 1928 and 1929, which would result in the odd shape and random layout of the building. In 1928, a long, narrow wooden structure was built next door to serve as a three-car garage, but it was converted to serve as a pewter forge as part of the factory by the mid-1930s.[111] In later years, this space became known as the playhouse, where events could move indoors when the weather did not cooperate. Eleanor is said to have used the space to occasionally hold dances.

Eleanor worked hard to get the word out about the Val-Kill Industries project, and she was a great salesperson. She sold the furniture from a small showroom at her family's townhouse on East Sixty-Fifth Street to big names

A view inside the factory building at Val-Kill. *Roosevelt-Vanderbilt National Historic Site.*

like Vassar College and Sloane's department store.[112] Her work paid off, and they soon had more orders than they could handle. Landolfa helped bring a few more craftsmen into the factory to keep up with demand. When FDR became president, several pieces of Val-Kill furniture made their way to the White House at FDR's request. On the back of a photograph of himself, FDR wrote a little verse for Nancy: "In the Val-Kill Shop they say, Nan has hidden safe away, so the little birds declare, one large Presidential chair."[113] Later in 1927, the addition of Otto Berge added to the talented staff. He brought a desire to be as authentic as possible when it came to re-creating the eighteenth-century American designs.

As the factory continued to prosper, a few more ideas were added, including the forge for making pewter and other metal objects. This project was overseen by Otto's brother Arnold, who joined the factory in 1929. Once again, they made items similar to colonial patterns, along with some modern-day items like matchboxes and lamps. And finally, the idea for a weaving project had been considered for some time, and Eleanor's housekeeper, Nellie Johannsen, was sent to Asheville, North Carolina, to learn from Fred Seeley's homespun operations. Eleanor hoped that they could get a series of classes to teach anyone from the area the art of weaving homemade cloth. She financially assisted Nellie with the opening of a tearoom and gas station, which was located near the entrance to Val-Kill on Violet Avenue. In the back room of the tea shop, Nellie operated the loom, where she wove an average of eight hundred yards of cloth per year.[114] Sadly, they did not do as well as they hoped when it came to teaching locals, mostly because there weren't many people who desired to make their own clothes anymore. The building was still largely intact until 2017, when an explosion in a portion that had been turned into a restaurant destroyed the northern half of what used to be the tearoom. It has since reopened as a patio restaurant.

The factory operated for about nine years, but it is quite clear based on the orders that were coming in that their greatest saleswoman was also their best costumer. Eleanor placed orders for herself, FDR and her friends, but by the 1930s, the Depression had taken its toll on small operations like Val-Kill, and most people could not afford to spend the extra money on handcrafted items. The industries at Val-Kill never made much of a profit, and it was decided in May 1936 that the partners, Eleanor, Marion, Nancy and Caroline, would hand over the operations to Otto Berge. The *New York Times* wrote, "Under the new arrangement the shop will be moved from the quarters occupied on the Roosevelt estate to the Berg home on Violet Avenue."[115] Berg would continue to run the business until right around the beginning of World War II.

After the industry was moved from the factory building, Eleanor decided it was time to break out on her own. Beginning in 1936, the factory building slowly morphed into a home of sorts. Eleanor decided that she would have a section to herself and a little apartment for her devoted secretary, Malvina Thompson, or "Tommy," as everyone called her. Tommy and her partner, Henry Osthagen, helped Eleanor redesign the space into a comfortable home.[116] Henry brought in local woodworkers and masons from Poughkeepsie to help with the project, though the layout of the home is far from ideal, with more bedrooms than bathrooms, tiny kitchens in both Eleanor's and Tommy's sides and narrow and dark staircases that feel like they belong in the servants' wing in Springwood. To top it off, the front door where she received all of her guests is actually at the back of the house.

Her niece Eleanor, the daughter of her little brother, Hall, once wrote, "Perhaps Aunt Eleanor lacked a clear idea of what the dimensions of the rooms might be, or could not imagine from looking at the blueprints how the actual spaces would work out; in any case, it is not a designer's dream of a house."[117] While it is true that the spaces seem odd, Eleanor made it feel like a livable home more than any other place she had ever lived. She quickly filled her new private spaces with furniture, prints, books and various gifts she had received.

For Eleanor though, what was even more important than the material items were the new people she had in her life. As first lady, she was developing new and exciting friendships, and while the changes clearly made her happy, this was also the sign of the end of her friendship with Marion and Nancy. The two people who had once been the most important part of her world were fading into the background of an overpopulated cast of characters ranging from the political world all the way to Hollywood. Marion and Nancy tolerated much of the madness—the scores of press and wild parties that trampled their beloved gardens. But some of the new people in Eleanor's life, like Tommy and journalist Lorena "Hick" Hickok, they simply could not learn to love as she did. Hick, on the other hand, considered both Marion and Nancy to be "self-absorbed snobs."[118]

As time went on, Marion and Nancy noticed that not only were there too many people around, but also instead of the three of them being mentioned together in the press as a team in their various projects, most of the time, it was just the first lady getting the credit. They had become a footnote in the life of the woman they had helped become stronger. Meanwhile, Eleanor resented that the two of them claimed they did all of this work just to make Eleanor the woman she was. She insisted, instead, that she wanted to help both of them accomplish their dreams—Nancy with her factory and Marion with her school.

Val-Kill, the factory building showing Eleanor's additions to make it a home. *Photo taken by the author.*

The words between the three of them became harsher as the 1930s went on, and as tempers flared, little things seemed to bother Eleanor all the more. Sadly, in 1938, Eleanor finally lost her patience, and she and Nancy had it out in what became known as "a long and tragic talk." The honeymoon had ended and turned into what could only be seen as a long and painful divorce.[119] Over the course of the next several months, the three women would battle it out through written message to determine how they would split the use of Val-Kill. By November, they had signed an agreement in which Marion and Nancy would continue to live in the cottage and Eleanor would have the factory building, paying the two former friends $1,000 a year for the next ten years to settle their contributions.[120]

When FDR died in 1945, Eleanor began the process of moving personal belongings from the White House and the "big house," and she took great joy in organizing things at Val-Kill just the way she wanted. It was truly the first time she could decorate as she saw fit. She moved items into her bedroom on the second floor and decided to use the sleeping porch as her main bedroom, at least as long as the weather permitted.

She kept FDR's Scottish terrier, Fala, with her as her new and faithful companion, and he had a bed on the sleeping porch next to hers. In the mornings, she would walk him through the woods. She even took him with her whenever she went to Springwood for special visits. On one occasion, she had forgotten his leash and put him down when she entered the front door of Springwood, and before the guards could grab him, he dashed up the stairs. After searching for him for some time, they found Fala "on the foot of the President's bed," where he had most certainly slept alongside his master many times before.[121]

By 1946, the big house was no longer the family headquarters but was a busy tourist attraction for loyal Roosevelt fans. Family and political operations soon migrated to Val-Kill, where as far as Marion and Nancy could see, the size of the crowds seemed to double with politicians, activists and an endless stream of family and grandchildren. Eleanor's regular visitors included over a dozen grandchildren by now, countless cousins and her children's spouses and ex-spouses, who still considered themselves part of the family. Elliott Roosevelt had also moved into Top Cottage, and he and his mother were planning farming operations on the rest of the property.

In the course of their agreement, Marion, Nancy and Eleanor had determined that they would share the use of the lawns, gardens and pool. However, Nancy was growing tired of Eleanor's grandchildren, adult children and dogs leaving a mess around the pool and in her beloved gardens. She

Val-Kill, showing the stone cottage in the springtime. *Photo taken by the author.*

Eleanor taking Fala for a walk around the pond at Val-Kill, 1947. *Franklin D. Roosevelt Library and Museum.*

said, "I do not see the necessity for grown-ups to play games on the lawn since it invariably means rough playing and the throwing of things in the beds thereby breaking flowers and shrubs which I have nursed for years."[122]

It did not take long for Marion and Nancy to finally come to the conclusion that it was time to leave Hyde Park. What had once been such a loving and perfect friendship, with hopes and dreams of making the world a better place for education, workers and Democratic women, had officially and bitterly come to an end. In August 1947, the three "graces of Val-Kill" agreed on the sum of $17,500 for Marion and Nancy to be bought out of their interests on the property and the stone cottage.[123] Nancy wrote to Eleanor to inform her of the day they were planning to leave and that they would hand over the keys to her if she was at home. Eleanor decided to make herself unavailable for their departure.

FDR's death meant a whole new series of financial complications for Eleanor and the children. Since the trustees of FDR's estate interpreted the contents of his will to mean that the land had to be sold rather than just given away, Eleanor decided to purchase land around her Val-Kill property. In 1947, she purchased 832 acres for $85,000 and then signed it over to her son Elliott for the purpose of "entering into the business of farming."[124] Eleanor and Elliott saw that FDR's tree plantations could make some money, and they worked closely with FDR's forestry consultant, Nelson Brown, informing him of their wishes to continue the Christmas tree business. For a few years, the Christmas trees were doing well, and Eleanor boasted about selling the trees in New York City in her My Day column. In 1948, Elliott expanded the Val-Kill farms by adding chickens and turkeys to the operation, and he showed interest in pursuing a cattle farm on the property as well, but by 1949, Elliott was losing interest in the project as he pursued other interests, such as the movie theaters that he built across the street from Springwood. But his life was also filled with complications at the time, as his wife, actress Faye Emerson, caught a plane to Mexico City to divorce him by 1950.[125]

For a few years, Eleanor had used the stone cottage as a guest house, until her youngest son, John, showed interest in living there. In 1951, John; his first wife, Anne Lindsay Clark; and their children, Haven, Anne and Sara, moved into the stone cottage. John made minor changes to the house to accommodate his family, which would grow by one more child, a daughter named Joan, the following year. He changed the layout of the second floor to split it into bedrooms and added a laundry room on the back of the house. John also bought out Elliott's interest in the Val-Kill properties as Elliott made his way to Miami Beach.

John took over the role that had belonged to Eleanor's secretary, Tommy, when she died in 1953—not that of taking dictation and keeping Eleanor's schedule straight but of mixing drinks at a very brief cocktail hour before dinner. Tommy's little kitchen just off of the living room in her portion of the factory was rarely used for cooking. It had always been known as Tommy's "cocktail closet," but John was usually able to convince his mother to let the cocktail hour go just a little bit longer than Tommy ever could.[126] Eleanor was rarely present for the better part of cocktail hour, and she tried to stay away from most drinking, since both her father and her brother Hall died from alcoholism. John also took over the role of overseeing Eleanor's staff and the general care of the property.

Eleanor took over what had once been Tommy's living room to use as her office space. Henry Osthagen still lived in one of the bedrooms just next door. In Eleanor's later years, when guests were invited into the home, the office was usually the first stop, especially if one was coming for dinner. Guests could sit on the couch and see Eleanor's desk, where a nameplate that had been given to her as a gift sat, even though her name was misspelled.[127] Drinks and conversation would be held briefly in the office, while Eleanor's cooks worked in the tiny kitchen beside the dining room.

In 1956, Eleanor's main groundskeeper and all-around handyman, Charles Curran, asked a local to help with one of Eleanor's Memorial Day picnics. Lester Entrup had no idea what he was getting into. When he saw the huge crowds of people who went to parties at Val-Kill, it was quite a shock. Les and his wife, Marge Entrup, had both operated a tavern in Hyde Park when they had fallen on hard times. However, after Les helped with the picnic in 1956, Eleanor asked the two of them to be her cooks, and they and their children could live at Val-Kill.[128]

During their first night on the job at Val-Kill, Marge and Les discovered that Eleanor tended to bring more people to dinner than she had planned. Years later, Les told the National Park Service that he "had to cut the roast so thin you could see through it" just to make it go around.[129] Marge proclaimed that she almost quit when, after only being on the job for a week, Eleanor informed them that they would be cooking for Haile Selassie, the emperor of Ethiopia.[130] Marge was not accustomed to dealing with royalty, but when the emperor arrived, his biggest concern seemed to be the chance to watch himself on TV, which was located in the office just opposite the fireplace and the desk where Eleanor worked. Marge and Les would have to get used to the many important visitors who they would prepare meals for, including Nikita Khrushchev, who only had time for one of Marge's dinner rolls, in

Above: Eleanor on her sleeping porch at Val-Kill with Tamas McFala and his grandfather, Fala, lying in his bed. *Franklin D. Roosevelt Library and Museum.*

Opposite, top: Eleanor uses the grill on her back porch at Val-Kill, 1938. *Franklin D. Roosevelt Library and Museum.*

Opposite, bottom: Eleanor with her guests in the dining room at Val-Kill, 1962. *Franklin D. Roosevelt Library and Museum.*

1959 and John F. Kennedy, who came not for the food but for Eleanor's political support, in 1960.[131]

The dining room was small and had a large walnut table with many leaves in the center. Eleanor had a set of silver that she brought out for special occasions. Many of the pieces were antiques that had been passed down over time. Eleanor was not the sort to buy fancy things for herself, and there wasn't much in the way of fine china at the table. She preferred Franciscan Ware, particularly the apple pattern, but it was quite common to find paper plates in use for larger gatherings. Eleanor enjoyed telling the story of a French madame at Versailles who used paper plates at a party to the confusion of her guests and insisted, "But, of course, everyone is using paper plates. Its all the rage! Just like Madame Roosevelt."[132]

Hanging from the windows near the kitchen are two stained-glass medallions, which were handcrafted by C.J. Connick, who also made the windows for the Cathedral of St. John the Devine in New York. These were gifts to FDR, who helped with the fundraising campaign for the church, but Eleanor kept them in her home, and they are still on display today.[133]

Besides world leaders and family, Eleanor was also delighted to have people from every background and circumstance at her home. She was especially fond of children who were less fortunate than her own. The Wiltwyck School for Boys had been a longtime interest of Eleanor's, and she loved to entertain the boys, sometimes more than one hundred of them at a time. The boys would be sent over in buses from their school just across the river for an annual summer picnic at Val-Kill. Eleanor liked to gather her grandchildren to help serve the boys hot dogs, salads and ice cream.[134] No matter who the guest might be, Eleanor was always the most gracious of hosts, doing whatever she could to make everyone feel at home.

By the end of her life, Eleanor was still staying busy between work and family. She would occasionally entertain the idea of retiring to sit by the fire and knit her final days away, but none of her children took that seriously. Her income was well over $100,000 in 1961, thanks to her writing, lectures and teaching.[135] She even took on several projects from President John F. Kennedy that year. By 1960, she had twenty grandchildren and more than a dozen great-grandchildren who kept her busy, especially shopping for Christmas. All of the children knew that there was a closet down the hall from Eleanor's second-floor bedroom where the presents would accumulate over the course of the year, and they would sometimes sneak a peek to see which boxes might be theirs. In 1962, she traveled to Europe and Israel before finally slowing down in the last couple of months of her life. Not long after informing her friend and physician Dr. David Gurewitsch that she had no desire to live if she could no longer be of use to people, Eleanor passed away in her townhouse in Manhattan on November 7, 1962.

Her dear friend and biographer Joseph Lash wrote about her devotion to the people of Hyde Park in his work *Eleanor: The Years Alone*, saying that she was well aware of the importance of the Roosevelt history to the town, and the town had meant so much to both her and FDR. But Eleanor never thought to save her house for history's sake—or perhaps she did not believe that people would flock to take a tour of her home, at least not like they did for FDR. Val-Kill was not left to the National Park Service like Springwood was.

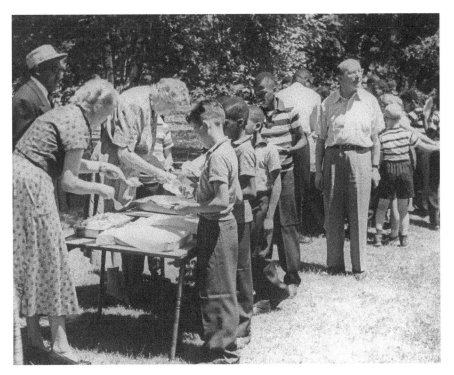

Eleanor serves hot dogs and salads to the children from the Wiltwyck School for Boys. *Franklin D. Roosevelt Library and Museum.*

When Eleanor died, her son John and his family were still living in the stone cottage. He converted his mother's home into four rental apartments and the playhouse building, formerly the forge, into one.[136] In 1970, on the anniversary of her death, John and his wife held an auction at Val-Kill, selling off the contents of his mother's home. One resident made off with one of FDR's steamer trunks with his initials on the side for fifty cents. By 1971, ads could be found in the *Poughkeepsie Journal* for the Val-Kill estate. John was ready to sell.

Drs. Rosario G. Dolce and William J. Squires of Long Island purchased the estate for $211,000. The doctors attempted to apply for a zoning change on the property to allow them to create condominiums for seniors, but they were turned down. In 1972, Eleanor Roosevelt wings were dedicated at FDR's presidential library, but many locals felt that more could be done to memorialize one of the most powerful first ladies in the world. By the mid-1970s, a grassroots movement was formed in a town of mostly Republicans to save the home of their neighbor, who was more than just a liberal Democrat,

Eleanor reads to the boys from the Wiltwyck School on June 19, 1954. *Franklin D. Roosevelt Library and Museum.*

she was a friend. By May 1977, both the House of Representatives and Senate passed a bill allowing over $500,000 in funds for land acquisition and over $400,000 for improvements for the site. Dubbed Eleanor Roosevelt National Historic Site, Val-Kill became the first national park dedicated to a first lady.[137]

Over the years, the National Park Service, with the help of partners like the Roosevelt-Vanderbilt Historical Association, the Eleanor Roosevelt Val-Kill Partnership and the Eleanor Roosevelt Center at Val-Kill, have endeavored to bring the houses and gardens back to the way Mrs. Roosevelt had them.[138] Though most of her personal collections were sold at auction, many of the objects have found their way back over the years, either through gracious gifts or loans, and are on display in the home just as Eleanor had them, right down to the misspelled nameplate on her original desk. The pool has been restored, along with her tennis court and the stone grilling pit where many picnics were enjoyed. Today, the park receives thousands of visitors and schoolchildren, who come from all over the world to learn about her endless passion for people just like us. If she were alive today, she would, no doubt, invite each of us to stay for a hot dog.

11

TOP COTTAGE

FDR had many titles during the course of his life, including state senator, assistant secretary of the navy, New York governor, historian, president and, perhaps surprisingly, architect. FDR considered himself a bit of an amateur architect by putting his thoughts and sketches into several of the buildings that popped up around Hyde Park during his lifetime. He was a lover of early Dutch Colonial architecture and worked with his friend and fellow local historian Helen Wilkinson Reynolds to study the local houses that dated to the eighteenth century. His passion for early stone buildings came through in several of the buildings he contributed to the town of Hyde Park, including three schools, a post office and his own presidential library. Even his wife's cottage at Val-Kill is inspired by that early architecture. But it is his own little place atop a hillside where we can see the true architect shine through in our thirty-second president.

FDR had essentially lived in other people's homes for most of his life. When he was senator and assistant secretary of the navy, he rented places in Albany and Washington, and even as president, the White House belonged to the people, not to him. His mother made it clear that she was in control of Springwood, and even the townhouse in Manhattan was planned and paid for by Sara. Both of these places overflowed with people who wanted to carve out some time with the president, resulting in a sea of characters who he lovingly referred to as the "mob." With all of this and the troubles of the world weighing down on him, FDR longed for a place where he could

FDR holds on to Fala on his porch at Top Cottage, 1941. *From the collections at Wilderstein Historic Site.*

escape from the crowds and focus on his own hobbies of stamp collecting, model ships, birding and reading.

One afternoon in 1935, FDR took his cousin and confidant Daisy Suckley on a drive through the country roads of Hyde Park. His afternoon drives through the back roads of the countryside were his way of escaping the mob, and Daisy was his quiet friend who he could vent to. He never had to worry about his thoughts being repeated by her lips. On this drive, they ended up on top of what locals in Hyde Park called Dutchess Hill, where they parked and talked quietly about the future. FDR explained that he had been hoping that one day he could buy this property and build some kind of "lean-to shelter with a fireplace and kitchenette" on this lovely overlook.[139]

Daisy and the president wrote to each other over the course of the next few years with plans to create a place where FDR would retire, and Daisy, with FDR's encouragement, envisioned herself as part of that retirement. They both referred to the spot as "our hill." Daisy even went so far as to send the president sketches of what she felt the site should look like. She wrote to him on September 11, 1935, in a style that was becoming more and more flirtatious with each passing letter: "After much thought I have come to the very definite conclusion that OUR HILL is, quite without exception, the nicest hill in Dutchess County! The only problem remaining is as to how it should be spelled, Just plain Our-Hill or OURHILL, or Owahill, or even OW-WA-HILL!"[140]

Between 1935 and 1938, FDR was able to purchase the property that he needed around the Dutchess Hill area. He had been eyeing the Dumphy farm, which had belonged to his neighbors, first Thomas

Daisy Suckley standing at Top Cottage. *From the collections at Wilderstein Historic Site.*

Newbold and then later his daughter, Mary Newbold Morgan. It wasn't until 1935 that FDR was finally able to make a deal with Mrs. Morgan to buy a portion of the farm for $1,000. He later worked with Jeff Newbold to buy the remainder of the farm and the Hughson farm, bringing his added land to 276.5 acres. The entire deal cost him $21,000.[141] During this time, the president was also making deals and swapping parcels of land with his friend and publisher Dorothy Schiff Backer, who he had convinced to buy land on top of Dutchess Hill and build a country home of her own. The *Poughkeepsie Journal* reported the deal in the real estate section in November 1938 and referred to him as "President Roosevelt, squire of Hyde Park and first citizen of the land."[142]

The original idea of a lean-to morphed into the mention of a log cabin. Daisy wrote to FDR asking if a log cabin was what he had wished for. "I don't think so," he replied and referred to other log cabins that just looked "very artificial" and full of "crawly bugs."[143] He suggested a stone cottage with two rooms and just one level, similar to that of his Beekman ancestors. By 1937, FDR and Daisy started a series of sketches that would essentially be the future of "our cottage," as they called it. Daisy was working on the floorplans and the placement of the furniture. Her feelings for the president were very clear, and it appears that FDR thoroughly enjoyed the attention he received from women like Daisy who showed him the same sort of devotion that his mother had.

By 1938, FDR had decided that this cottage would be used only seasonally. He planned to spend his winters in Georgia as he had for many years. His little cottage in Warm Springs had brought him through some of the toughest years of his life, and although the setting was quite different from his Hudson Valley home, he could always rely on finding peace there. He told Daisy that he might spend the occasional winter afternoon in the new place on the hill, but it would not be a year-round home. If one walks up the path through the woods, which is similar to the road that FDR would have driven, it is easy to see that getting to the cottage when there is too much snow would be quite difficult.

At some point in 1937, FDR had reached out to Henry Toombs, who had worked with the Roosevelts on various projects, including Val-Kill cottage and the James Roosevelt Memorial Library, which Sara had given to the Town of Hyde Park in 1927. Toombs considered FDR's plans for the cottage to be very well done and even suggested that the president's name should be put on the drawings as the architect of the project, while Henry would be listed as associate. Toombs joked in a letter to Marguerite LeHand that even though he wasn't licensed to practice architecture in New York, they shouldn't get into any trouble for it; however, "as to just how we would split the fee is another matter which I would have to discuss with him later."[144]

The first estimates for the construction of the cottage were from $18,000 to well over $20,000, which the president made clear to Toombs he could not possibly afford. Finally, an offer from Adams-Faber Company from Montclair, New Jersey, was made in 1938 to do the work for $16,599.[145] FDR took pleasure in overseeing every part of the construction of the house. Whenever he could, he would drive up to visit the progress, and his caretaker, Christian Bie, would write to him with updates and suggestions. Paul Adams and John Faber, who did the construction work, wrote to FDR's secretary saying they never worked with a client more interested in every aspect of the work before: "We would like to have the President know that we appreciate his helpful advice and suggestions."[146] What remains to be seen is whether or not this was their sincere thought. Work began in July 1938, and by October, they were already beginning the work of plastering the interior.

Electric was needed for the house, but there were no electric lines going into the woods where the cottage was located. At the time, the Central Hudson and Gas Company charged its costumers for pole installation, but FDR was determined to save money in any way he could. Since he

FDR sits in his custom Ford and admires the progress that has been made at Top Cottage, 1938. *Franklin D. Roosevelt Library and Museum.*

had his own tree farm, he saved money by providing seventeen poles for the electric lines.[147] The project seemed to be running more or less on budget, with the exception of an additional cost of a furnace, which FDR had not taken very seriously, as he did not think he would be spending large amounts of time at the house in the winter. The last payments to the contractors were made in January 1939, with the total amount coming to $17,086.25.[148]

The press latched on to FDR's project almost immediately after they heard of the plan. FDR did insist on showing them the progress and keeping them up to date but always referred to it as just "a little cottage." The press, on the other hand, dubbed it the "President's Dream House," much to the dismay of FDR. Whether it was coming from the press or his Hyde Park neighbors, it didn't matter who said it, he despised it. His secretary, Missy LeHand, even took the time to write to one of the workers to remind the plumbers, "Will you ask them please never call the cottage Roosevelt Dream House? The president speaks of it as The Hill Cottage."[149]

The crown prince and princess of Denmark are the first visitors to be entertained at Top Cottage. Notice the mismatched furniture, 1939. *Franklin D. Roosevelt Library and Museum.*

Aside from the bad nickname for his beloved new home, FDR was exposed to negative reactions from the world of professional architects, who did not like that Henry Toombs allowed FDR to be considered the lead architect on the project. When the drawings of the cottage were released, showing FDR as architect and Toombs as associate, John Lloyd Wright, son of Frank Lloyd Wright, stated how disappointed he was: "After seeing the title Architect after F.D. Roosevelt in your magazine, I give up.... The moral breakdown of the integrity and dignity of the Architectural profession seems now complete."[150] None of this really mattered to FDR. He was the only president besides Thomas Jefferson to design a building for his personal estate during his presidency, and now, he had a place that he could really call his own.

The first parties held at Top Cottage were modest. A photograph from May 1939, showing the first gathering with the crown prince and princess of Denmark, reveals that none of the furniture matched, and many members of the party used folding chairs. FDR would, in fact, never get around to fully furnishing the house. In 1939, he told the press, "It will probably get furnished over—I do not know what—ten or twelve years."[151] His caretaker, Christian Bie, who happened to be a cabinetmaker, designed several bookcases and tables for the house.

Over time, FDR would begin to fill the home with knickknacks, books, prints and, of course, all of the necessary tools for making a good martini. By 1944, Daisy wrote in her diary about the progress being made in furnishing the home: "Pictures were hung in all the first-floor rooms & the Chinese porcelain screen fastened to the wall. That little house is a little museum in itself." She went on to say that FDR was going to have everything inside of it catalogued.[152]

He took great joy in being able to entertain on his own without the help of others. The house was wheelchair accessible, with wide hallways and no thresholds in any of the doorways. He had a small table where he would mix and serve his cocktails and personally butter pieces of toast for anyone who wished—all with a smile and a story to tell. Daisy insisted that you hadn't truly lived until you'd had a piece of buttered toast made by FDR.

His greatest party in the cottage took place in the summer of 1939, when King George VI and his wife, Queen Consort Elizabeth, came to Hyde Park to stay for the weekend. The couple stayed in the big house, where the bedrooms were adequate and at least furnished, but they spent an afternoon at the cottage. This was the first visit to the United States for a serving English monarch, and FDR insisted on showing them his little retreat in the woods. Daisy wrote in her diary on Sunday, June 11, about how excited she and everyone in Hyde Park were to see the royal couple in all of their glory. After attending a church service at St. James, the party made its way up the hillside to the cottage for cold salads, cold beers and hot dogs. The royals got a sense for true American food. FDR even managed to sneak in some of his jokes with the king, to which "the King rocked back & forward with laughter."[153]

Years later, Eleanor recalled that FDR had refused to screen in his lovely porch, which proved to be a problem in the summer, when the mosquitos came out. Though FDR appeared to be immune to the nasty critters, many of his guests were not. On one visit, Queen Wilhelmina of the Netherlands was assaulted by the bugs. When she mentioned it to the president, he proclaimed that it simply wasn't possible, saying, "We don't have mosquitos here, they just don't exist." Eleanor was well aware of the fact that they did exist and were doing a great deal of damage to the queen's legs. She went into the cottage and brought back a blanket so that the queen could cover up. FDR paid no attention. Eleanor was never quite sure if it was FDR's polio that prevented him from noticing the bites, or if he just really never wanted to admit that his porch could do with a screen.[154]

Daisy witnessed not only the royal picnic but also an important meeting with FDR and Prime Minister Winston Churchill that took place in 1942. FDR had asked Daisy to serve tea for his guests at the cottage on June 21, which made her very nervous, but she managed to pull it off while listening to the important conversations concerning Germany's interests in developing an atomic bomb. One of the great gifts of Daisy and FDR's friendship is that she had the good sense to write down much of what she heard and saw while in the presence of the man she adored. She witnessed history being made, from the beginnings of the Manhattan Project to the outpourings of a man who had the world on his shoulders and was growing tired. A couple of months after the meeting with Churchill, she wrote about how she and FDR drove around Hyde Park alone. They stopped first at Crumwold, where she no doubt remembered the first time that she saw him dance. Then they headed to the cottage, where they sat, and she listened to him talk of his past as the sun went down—a moment of deep and quiet reflection that was rare for him to be able to enjoy.[155]

Even with all of the quiet afternoons and casual parties at Top Cottage, and even though the press referred to it as his "dream home," FDR would never spend a single night in Top Cottage. There have been many theories over the years as to why he never managed to officially make Top Cottage his home. Some say that his mother requested that he never live there during her lifetime, but since she passed away in 1941, there were several years where he might have had the chance. There was a rumor that Top Cottage did not have a telephone, which FDR had started himself when he told the press, "There isn't any telephone in the place…because, you know, if there's a telephone, somebody is sure to use it."[156] One cannot quite perform the duties of the president without access to the outside world, so it could be argued that the lack of a telephone was his reason for not staying overnight. However, telephone lines were installed in the house during construction, so that would be quite easy to fix. Perhaps he simply believed that he shouldn't call Top Cottage home until he finished his fourth term in office and retired from public service. Whatever the true reason, FDR never made Top Cottage his permanent residence. He died on April 12, 1945, not near his beloved Hudson River but in what he considered to be his second home, the "Little White House" in Warm Springs, Georgia.

FDR's remains were returned home to Hyde Park and laid to rest in his mother's rose garden near Springwood on April 15. Less than a month later,

Daisy was sent to Top Cottage to conduct an inventory of its collections. At the time, Daisy had been working at FDR's presidential library, and part of her work was organizing the president's personal papers. It was emotionally difficult to walk the house with her notepad and pen, jotting down each item and its importance. As she did, she could not help but take note of the many items that she had lent to him. Daisy knew when she stood in the house in May 1945 that it would be the last time she would have a chance to be alone in the place that she and the president dreamed about together. Almost all of the items left in the house were sold at auctions by Eleanor and Elliott Roosevelt in 1951.[157]

Elliott Roosevelt moved into the house just after the war ended. He and his wife, Faye Emerson, made it a home for the four children Elliott brought into the marriage from two previous marriages. They were technically the first and only Roosevelts to live in Top Cottage. During this time, Elliott did not make many changes to the house, with the exception of closing in the porch to add an additional living space. It wouldn't be his home for long, though. Elliott and Faye divorced in 1950. With his new desire to head south and invest in new business ventures, Elliott decided it was time to sell Top Cottage and some of the land around it. Some historians debate whether or not Eleanor was consulted on the matter of selling the house and that she woke up one morning to read the paper with the headline, "The Dream House of Roosevelt Sold." But she agreed to sell off the home's collections, and in the end, she generally defended Elliott's actions, regardless of whether or not she liked them.[158]

In December 1952, the house was purchased by Philip S. Potter, who moved in with his wife and son, though the name on the deed of the house was that of his wife, Agnes F. Potter. The Potter family took very good care of Top Cottage, with three different generations of the family calling it home. They did not make any major alterations to the bulk of house, with the exception of a few minor alterations on the property and the addition of a shed, which is still standing on the hillside just south of the house. However, Potter's sons did sell off much of the land surrounding the house during the course of the 1960s and '70s. This became known as Val-Kill Heights, and as a result, many modern houses have been constructed on the lands surrounding FDR's once-secluded retreat.[159]

The Potter family finally put the house up for sale in the early 1990s, which got the attention of members of the Roosevelt family, as well as various preservation groups. The property, which included the house and thirty-seven acres of land, was purchased by the Beaverkill Conservancy,

Top Cottage today. *Photo taken by the author.*

an affiliate of the Open Space Institute, for $750,000 in grants. Another $750,000 in restoration was needed to conserve the house and bring it up to standards to allow for visitation. The Franklin and Eleanor Roosevelt Institute worked with the Open Space Institute in overseeing the care of the house before turning it over to the National Park Service for continued operations.

In June 2001, tours began to make their way up to the cottage, which was still mostly empty. There are still very few objects in the house other than some reproductions made to look like some of the items that FDR once placed throughout the living room. The tour atmosphere is more of a conversation on Roosevelt history, which is led by National Park Service interpreters, and visitors are encouraged to take a seat on the porch where FDR once invited his guests to sit half a century ago.

Laura Delano's Evergreen Lands

Heading north on the Albany Post Road, there is a long stretch of open fields that once belonged to families like the Dinsmores, Livingstons and Mills. You'll pass through Staatsburg, which is considered part of the town of Hyde Park, with a few churches, a post office and a library, which was originally a church. Eventually, you'll come into the lands and village of Rhinebeck. Both Eleanor and FDR had several cousins connected with the old families, like the Livingstons and Astors. Eleanor was a descendent of Robert R. Livingston, also known as the Chancellor, who helped draft the Declaration of Independence. FDR's relatives on the Delano side of the family had married into the Astor clan and found themselves owning land around the edges of the town of Rhinebeck.

FDR's first cousin Laura Delano was considered by many to be the most eccentric of the family. She had earned the nickname "Polly" as a child, when she refused to drink any water other than Apollinairis Water, which was an imported carbonated beverage. She was born in 1885, the daughter of Warren Delano III and Jennie Walters of Baltimore. Laura grew up with her five siblings at Steen Valetje, a house her father had inherited from his uncle Franklin Hughes Delano. Laura and FDR's backgrounds were the same. They both had the same sense of entitlement and the feeling that they belonged by their beloved Hudson River. They had spent a good deal of time together as children, either at the Delano homes in Newburgh or Fairhaven, Massachusetts, or spending time sailing at Campobello.

Laura "Aunt Polly" Delano as a teenager. *Franklin D. Roosevelt Library and Museum.*

As an adult, Laura could always be counted on to shock those around her. She managed to color her hair a light purple by the 1930s and drew a dark widow's peak at the top of her forehead, which showed off her hair all the more. She was known for walking around her house in a silk dressing gown with several necklaces dangling from her neck and bracelets from her arm. Her clothing inspired some and horrified others. When she decided to paint her nails red, several women in the family remarked that she must have just "disemboweled a rabbit."[160] She was always surrounded by her championship-winning Irish setters or long-haired dachshunds, which she bred and showed at the Westminster Kennel Show. In fact, most of the newspapers, including the *New York Times*, simply referred to her as a "dog show judge," but to FDR, she was so much more.

Laura never married, most likely because the only love interest she ever had was a secretary of the Japanese Embassy, a former Harvard classmate of FDR's, Saburo Kurusu.[161] The idea of such a marriage was considered quite inappropriate by most of the family. She then decided to never marry. Instead, she kept an interesting assortment of affairs, supposedly with her chauffeur. She was famous for her fruity and potent cocktails and her ability to get all of the good gossip. FDR loved having her around for the entertainment and the friendship. Since she was unmarried, wealthy and devoted to nothing other than her dogs, Laura had the time to focus on her cousin and tag along on any adventure. She was invited along on several trips, including a few cross-country journeys to visit and inspect army camps and factories.

When FDR was home at Hyde Park, he almost always ate his meals at the Roosevelt estate, whether at his mother's home, Val-Kill or a lunch at Top Cottage. But there was one other house where he would eat the

Above: Laura with her prize-winning Irish setters on a Christmas card to Eleanor, 1945. *Franklin D. Roosevelt Library and Museum.*

Opposite: Laura with her puppies at the stone cottage, part of Foxhollow Farm, 1930. *Franklin D. Roosevelt Library and Museum.*

occasional dinner: Laura's beautiful home that he inspired her to build, Evergreen Lands.[162] Laura had lived at her father's home, Steen Valetje, surrounded by her family and her father's many horses, which no doubt inspired her own love for animals. Later, she rented the stone cottage on part of the Foxhollow estate, the home of the Dows family. This home was designed by Harrie Thomas Lindeberg and Lewis Colt Albro, both formerly employed by Stanford White, in 1907, and like many of the houses along the Hudson, its design paid tribute to the old eighteenth-century houses built of stone.[163]

By the early 1930s, Laura wanted a mansion to call her own. She brought in John Russell Pope, a nationally renowned architect, to design an English-style home with an Arts and Crafts feel. Pope was already a famed architect when he designed Evergreen Lands. He was born in New York City in 1874 and studied architecture at Columbia University. He was the first to win the Rome Prize and attend the American Academy in Rome, where he continued his studies. He also attended the École des Beaux-Arts in

Evergreen Lands today.
Photo taken by the author.

Paris, where he learned more about the popular Beaux-Arts style that many customers desired.[164]

Laura had over 150 acres of beautiful farmland that overlooked the valley and the Catskill Mountains to the west. Pope designed the house in the Tudor Revival style with a mix of stucco and local stone, perhaps at the suggestion of FDR and his insistence that the Dutch Colonial style not be forgotten.[165] The house has a beautiful, steep, multi-gabled roof, and Laura's initials are detailed into the copper gutters. The layout of the interior is cozy with smaller rooms but a grand living room with a fireplace and a kitchen that looks out over the backyard and the fabulous view seen from the patio below.

It was on this patio that FDR, Winston Churchill and Laura sat for what was supposed to be a tea but that turned into a cocktail hour, which was enjoyed by everyone except Churchill. Both Laura and FDR loved to mix cocktails and try new creations, but the very straightforward Churchill had asked for a straight Scotch. Laura, who did not like being turned down, decided that the prime minister should try one of her specialties instead and secretly mixed him a drink. When he took a sip from what he believed was a Scotch, he spat it out across her patio in anger. That was the last time the prime minister would visit Evergreen Lands.[166]

After FDR's death, Laura was the one to inform Eleanor of the fact that Lucy Mercer Rutherford, the woman FDR had an affair with so many years before, was in the room when FDR suffered his stroke.[167] Many believed that it was a harsh thing for her to do, but Laura believed that one way or another, Eleanor would figure it out. After the funeral at Hyde Park, Laura continued to live at Evergreen Lands, where she tended to her animals and continued her work in the dog show business.

She would later attend another funeral in Hyde Park, that of Eleanor Roosevelt's in 1962, where she stood amid a sea of mourners and held the arm of Governor Nelson Rockefeller, who walked her inside the church. Laura died in 1972 at the age of eighty-six. Since she had no children of her own, the contents of her home were sold in a large three-day auction in June 1972. The newspaper listing shows the estate contained everything from fine china to a Steinway baby grand piano to farm equipment. Her land was split into lots, and modern mini mansions have popped up along what is known as Delano Drive. Today, Laura's house is a private residence.

Daisy Suckley's Wilderstein

Whom FDR found himself in need of someone to talk to, he turned most willingly to his distant cousin and confidante Margaret "Daisy" Suckley. Daisy had been one of the many cousins known to the Roosevelt family who lived along the Hudson, but it was during FDR's turbulent years suffering from polio that he and Daisy began to connect on a friendly level. Within a year of being diagnosed with polio, FDR had exhausted many of those closest to him, including Eleanor, Louie Howe and even his mother. It was his mother who decided FDR needed someone else from outside those in the inner circle to confide in, and it had to be someone who could be trusted. He needed someone who wouldn't gossip about his issue and could happily listen to his jokes and stories without ever being judgmental or damaging to his already sensitive ego. Sara decided to reach out to Daisy, who could be all of these things, and as luck would have it, she was very close by.

Daisy had seen FDR a few times before. In 1910, she went to one of the famous New Year's Eve parties at Crumwold, the home of Archibald Rogers in Hyde Park. This massive mansion, designed by Richard Morris Hunt, was where FDR had once been tutored alongside his friends, the Rogers children. The highlight every year at Crumwold would be a glorious News Year's party with the Frank L. Schofield's Twenty-First Regimental Band providing the waltzes and members of New York's grand old families, including the Astors, Dinsmores, Chanlers and Roosevelts, in attendance.[168] Daisy was only eighteen when she first saw FDR, who was then twenty-eight and married with children. She would never forget this

Wilderstein from the northwest, showing the servants' wing. *From the collections of Wilderstein Historic Site.*

tall and handsome man with a wide smile who danced with grace around the room.[169] It is clear in Daisy's personal diary entries and her flirtatious correspondence with FDR that she had a crush on him since the moment she saw him that night.

Daisy lived just a few miles up the Albany Post Road outside the village of Rhinecliff in a beautiful Queen Anne home that the family called Wilderstein.

This is where she was born in 1891 and where she would spend most of her life until her death at the age of ninety-nine. The name for the home was inspired by a petroglyph just below the hill by the river's edge, which was referred to as "wild man's rock." The original house on the property had been established by Daisy's grandfather Thomas Suckley in 1852. The Suckley family could trace their heritage to some of the biggest names of the Hudson Valley, including the Livingstons, Beekmans and Schuylers. FDR and Daisy could claim that they both belonged, in some way, to all these grand old families.

It was Daisy's father Robert who decided to enlarge the house and bring it into a more fashionable design. Robert had inherited Wilderstein and a large fortune when his father died in February 1888. It did not take him long to find a suitable architect to transform the house into its current layout and grandness. Robert choose Arnout Cannon Jr. of Poughkeepsie along with his team of contractor brothers, Cornelius and George. Cannon had already developed several fine architectural achievements, and a few of his buildings still dot the streets of Poughkeepsie, including the Vassar Brother's Institute and the Masonic Temple. Cannon established himself after apprenticing under his father in the 1850s in the years before the United States had established its own school for architecture.

Cannon designed plans for the new Suckley home by May 1888, which were approved very quickly, allowing construction to begin that summer.[170] The house was changed dramatically from its very square original footprint to an asymmetrical creation of many dramatic angles, a five-story circular tower, spacious porches, a grand stairway and a conservatory. The house even had a state-of-the-art burglar alarm system, installed by George Cannon and attached to the first-floor windows, that would operate an alarm gong located on the second floor. Cannon also included an elaborate carriage house just down the hill from the house, as well as a boathouse, which was destroyed by fire in 1940.

Joseph Burr Tiffany, the cousin of Louis Comfort Tiffany, was hired to work with Suckley on the interior decorating, which cost even more than the work done to the exterior. The check stubs show Suckley spending well over $35,000 on the work that took place throughout 1889.[171] Each room was designed with a different style to give the house many layers and make it feel as if you were walking between time periods when walking between rooms, from Jacobean to Louis XVI. To top it all off, Suckley brought in Calvert Vaux, the acclaimed landscape architect, to update the grounds of the estate into a romantic country setting. Vaux also designed a lodge and

An early image of Wilderstein, showing a young Daisy Suckley with her brothers Arthur and Robert. *From the collections of Wilderstein Historic Site.*

placed several little gazebos in perfect locations along the property to take advantage of the glorious views.

Life at Wilderstein had its ups and downs. Daisy was the fourth of seven children who would call this place home, but they would not always be able to enjoy it to the fullest extent. Robert Suckley had a law practice in the city but rarely paid much attention to it after inheriting his father's wealth. He was not the only one of his class to have such a situation; James Roosevelt lived a similar lifestyle. However, this lack of new income would hurt the family's finances over time, especially in the years following the financial panic of 1893, forcing them not only to leave Wilderstein for several years but also to sell their townhouse in Manhattan.[172] Henry, Daisy's oldest oldest brother, lost his life while serving in the First World War, and Daisy watched as her two younger brothers, Robert and Arthur, decided to follow in her father's life of leisure, though there was not enough money to continue that life by the 1920s. Daisy found herself not only taking care of her family financially, with what odd jobs she could find, but also tending to the needs of her new friend FDR, which does not appear to have been a burden on her.

FDR certainly visited the house, where it is said he would receive massages to ease his suffering, but it was generally Daisy who would go to him. Almost every time FDR came home to Hyde Park during his presidency, Daisy would make an appearance. She also visited Washington a few times. Nobody ever seemed to mind her presence—not even Eleanor, as Daisy was known for her polite and quiet demeanor. Between the time spent together and the various gifts they gave to each other, their connection would always be important. One of FDR's other great friends in his later years was one of those gifts: his little Scottish terrier, Fala, which Daisy gave to him in 1940 after she had lovingly trained him to be a great companion.[173]

The friendship, which has been covered in detail by Roosevelt scholar Geoffrey C. Ward, would prove to save Daisy from some of her financial worries, when in September 1941, FDR hired her to work with the archivists in his new presidential library. He visited her at Wilderstein for tea to give her the good news. She would organize his personal papers and catalogue all of his collections and incoming gifts, sometimes working right alongside him. In her diary on September 13, 1943, she wrote, "He worked there for an hour and a half while I flew around getting things done, my desk piled high, two trucks and a table full of things waiting to be taken care of."[174] She

Daisy and a Scottish terrier admiring Wilderstein, 1957. *From the collections of Wilderstein Historic Site.*

would continue to work at the presidential library, helping researchers and historians write books that both honored her cherished friend and criticized him, until her retirement in 1963.[175]

Daisy and Laura Delano were part of the small group of people in the room when FDR lost consciousness and slipped from the world on April 12, 1945. The importance of the moment was not lost on Daisy, who had been worried about his health for well over a year. His doctors had asked him to cut down on the cigarettes and drinking and try to take his meals alone without the disturbance of guests asking questions and favors of him. However, the stress of the war had taken its toll, and Daisy was there to hear him proclaim, "I have a terrific pain at the back of my head" just before suffering a cerebral hemorrhage.[176] The loss of her friend caused her great pain, perhaps more than most, and though she spoke with countless historians until her death in 1991, she found it very difficult to talk about the final hours she spent with him.

Daisy had continued the never-ending battle of maintaining her old Victorian home until her death. The house had not been painted since 1910, and there were no longer any servants to aid her with the tasks of caring for the countless pieces of furniture and collections that had been accumulating for over a century, since the Suckley family never threw anything away. By the 1980s, Daisy had determined that her home needed to be preserved for history. It is quite possible that she was inspired by FDR's preservation of his own family's home. However, nobody famous had ever lived at Wilderstein, and it was not the only Queen Anne home in the Hudson Valley, so what made this house worthy of saving? It was the dedication of a few concerned citizens, including Daisy herself. "To me it is the perfect Victorian home from the cellar to the attic," she said. "It should all be preserved."[177]

Today, Wilderstein is open to visitors with guided tours of the house and hiking trails that span the property through the woods and meadows and down toward the Hudson. It is privately run by an organization that Daisy helped create, named Wilderstein Preservation. Since its opening, the exterior of the house has finally been repainted to its original bright red with dark forest green trim. Beginning in 2019, the first floor has been the focus of the tours, as electricity was limited to certain parts of the house. The second floor is in the process of being brought back to life, with the help of a dedicated staff who wish to do the house justice by getting all of the original details cleaned on everything from furnishings to doorknobs, as well as having all the wallpaper restored. The house is still filled with every piece of the Suckley family story. When Daisy died, a box was discovered under

Left: Wilderstein in desperate need of a paint job. *From the collections of Wilderstein Historic Site.*

Below: Stained-glass window from inside Wilderstein. *Photo taken by the author.*

her bed that contained all of the intimate letters between her and FDR, as well as the diary entries that she had sworn to historians for years that she didn't have. There was a reason she kept it all: she didn't want to forget, nor did she want anyone else to.

Steen Valetje

FDR's great-uncle Franklin Hughes Delano did well for himself in business and life. He had partnered with his brothers Warren and Frederick in the shipping business in the 1830s. He also joined the large New York shipping firm of Grinnell, Minturn and Company, where he managed to make a reasonable fortune. But perhaps his most profitable venture was his marriage to Laura Astor, the granddaughter of John Jacob Astor, in 1844.[178] This marriage would allow Franklin to retire by the age of thirty-one, and as a wedding present, the couple was gifted the large estate that adjoined John Jacob Astor's Rokeby. It was an old Dutch farm alongside the Hudson River called Steen Valetje, which means "little stone valley."[179]

In 1849, an agreement was made between Franklin Hughes Delano and British architect Frank Wills for the price of $14,500 for work to be completed on their new home. He also hired Meeker and Angevine to design the barn and wagon house at a cost of $3,700. Plumbing costs for the main house were estimated at around $450. Frank Wills wrote in his plans for the house that "all the mortar used in the building [is] to be of the best Kingston Lime and water gravel. The footings are to be 12 inches wider than their respective walls and are to be of the largest and squarest stones."[180] Wills also designed furniture specifically for the house, as well as custom floor tiles, as seen from the drawings located in the Delano family papers collection. Estimates for carpenters, masons and other various workers literally piled up between 1848 and 1849, but that did not seem to bother the Delanos, who had plenty of Astor money to play with. The firm of Wooley and

Modern view of
Steen Valetje.
*Photo taken by
Jonathon Simons from
Hudsonhometours.com.*

Hughes sent its bill for work on the gatehouse and stable to cost just over $3,000. Robert Pugsley was signed on as the carpenter, and Morgan Dayton worked as the mason. In 1874, Arthur B. Jennings won the contract for the construction of a carriage house.

In 1881, architect Thomas Stent was brought in to make alterations to the old house, including the addition of skylights, a dumbwaiter and cold air ducts. In the contract for the plumber there is an interesting addition of bells and speaking tubes that were to be put into the house. The bells were to be hung from the bedrooms to communicate with the servants' apartments, and speaking tubes were also to be placed in various locations to call on the servants with special instructions. The architect also wanted electric call bells in the dining room, parlors and the private office. A greenhouse was expanded with hotbeds, and a stonewall was completed. Between 1881 and 1882, the improvements made to the entire estate appear to have cost at least $113,007.01.[181] But this was small change to Franklin and Laura.

The records in the FDR Presidential Library show that the superintendent of the estate appears to have been William Anderson, as he paid the wages of the other employees, but he was paid directly from Franklin Hughes Delano, and his wages appear to have been quite good—nine months paid in full was $540 on September 25, 1893. This date was just a few months before the death of Franklin; he died in December of that year. While his brother Warren's household at Algonac was full of the sounds of screaming and laughing children, life at Steen Valetje was much quieter, as Franklin and Laura had no children of their own. In fact, they spent a good deal of time traveling and spoiling their nieces and nephews, as well as the younger generations. After Franklin died in France, his will shows that he was indeed quite wealthy, with a real estate value of over $90,000 and personal wealth over $1 million. Much of the wealth was split between various relatives, and

Above: Drawings by architect Frank Wills for furniture at Steen Valetje. *Franklin D. Roosevelt Library and Museum.*

Left: Interior of Steen Valetje, taken from an auction catalogue, 1970s. *Franklin D. Roosevelt Library and Museum.*

FDR and his mother were not left out—Franklin left his namesake $10,000, and his niece Sara received $100,000.[182] Of course, his wife would remain in control of Steen Valetje until her death in 1902 in Switzerland.

The house was then given to Franklin's brother's son Warren III, though he appears to have used the house as a summer residence for some time before Laura's death in 1902.[183] Warren was a well-educated young man. He was born in Newburgh at Algonac in 1852 and spent time learning in Hanover, Germany, as well as at Harvard. He earned a degree at the Lawrence Scientific School in 1874.[184] While at Harvard, he met and fell in love with Jennie Walters of Baltimore, the sister of Henry Walters, his friend and classmate. She was the daughter of William Thompson and Ellen Walters, whose art collection would become the foundations of the famous Walters Art Gallery in Baltimore.[185] Warren and Jennie had seven children, with five who survived into adulthood, including Laura Franklin Delano.

Warren's investments in coal mines in Pennsylvania, along with his inheritance, allowed him to focus much of his attention on his great passion, horses. The estate has a stable, where Warren could be found working with any of the sixty-five horses that he owned and showed at the local Dutchess County Fair, which included saddle, driving and heavy draft horses. In 1920, Warren had been appointed to serve as superintendent of the horse show for the fair and was working with his stablemen preparing, when he decided to take one of his horses for a drive to the train station just north of his home in Barrytown. He needed to pick up a trunk that was being delivered at the station, and in the process of securing the trunk to his carriage, his horse Belle was spooked by an oncoming train and ran right in front of it onto the tracks. The *New York Times* wrote in detail about what happened to Warren and his horse: "The train struck the buggy squarely in the middle and carried it 150 feet down the tracks." The article went on to say that when onlookers ran to the aid of Warren, he was still sitting in the mangled buggy, but his neck had broken instantaneously.[186]

After Warren's death, the house would be left to his son Lyman, who with his wife, Leila Burnett Delano, made some alterations to the house and changed its name to Mandara. Eleanor stopped by to visit Leila a few years after Lyman passed away in 1944, and she wrote about the house in her My Day column. "Steen Valetje, in spite of being built in the Victorian era, has more real charm and sense of being a house where people have lived and really understood and loved their possessions than some houses where you have a feeling that a perfectly impersonal decorator was called in to hang the curtains and lay the rugs."[187] Lyman and Leila were the

Left: Interior of Steen Valetje today. *Photo taken by Jonathon Simons from Hudsonhometours.com.*

Below: Modern view of Steen Valetje. *Photo taken by Jonathon Simons from Hudsonhometours.com.*

last of the Delanos to call this amazing place home. After Leila's death in 1966, the estate was put up for sale. An auction catalogue from the 1970s shows some of the interiors of the home with some of the furnishings that were made for the house.

Today, the estate is in private hands, with modern improvements including a massive pool and pool house. Some of the original details are still left in place, like the tiles in the front entryway, which were designed by the original architect, Frank Wills. When driving across the Kingston-Rhinecliff bridge, sometimes you can spot the modern pool house with its Doric temple appearance. The name of the estate has been changed again, as shown on the front gate beside the original gatehouse. It reads Atalanta. In 2020, the house was on the market, with ten bedrooms, ten bathrooms and over 144 acres. It had an asking price of $15 million. The estate remains one of the grandest private homes in the Hudson Valley.

Oak Terrace

E leanor Roosevelt's childhood was filled with anxiety and sadness. Even
when her parents were alive, she felt unsure of herself and was afraid
of everything including being a disappointment to her parents, sailing and
even the dark. After the deaths of her mother, brother Elliott and father,
she spent the rest of her life fighting off bouts of depression. Her dreams
of living a happy life with her father had come to a bitter end in 1894, and
now, at ten years old, she was left to tend to her little brother. Eleanor would
admit later in life that she felt as if she were a constant guest at each place,
with no home of her own for at least half of her life. Sadly, after the death
of her parents, she was now an orphan, drifting even further from a place
where she could feel at ease.

Both Eleanor and her brother Hall were sent to live with her
grandmother at her residences in the city and in Tivoli at Oak Lawn,
which Eleanor called Oak Terrace. The house was not as old as some of
the other Livingston homes nearby, but it was surrounded by history and
beauty. Eleanor's grandparents Mary Livingston Ludlow and Valentine G.
Hall Jr. had hired architect Carl Pfeiffer to design their home in 1872. It is
built of brick in the Second Empire style, which was popular at the time,
with the mansard roof as the third floor. The grounds swept down to the
Hudson, with unobstructed views of the Catskill Mountains. The mile-
long driveway leads out to a gatehouse and Woods Road, where if one
were to walk south, several driveways to other Livingston homes appear
one by one.

Oak Terrace, the home where Eleanor and her brother Hall spent much of their youth. *Franklin D. Roosevelt Library and Museum.*

Beginning in 1686, the land where this house now sits, as well as all of the others in the area, was part of the 160,000-acre property known as Livingston Manor.[188] Lord Robert Livingston and his wife, Alida Schuyler Van Rensselaer, oversaw the settling of tenant farmers here, and from the eighteenth century through the nineteenth century, decedents of the Livingston Lords built their mansions here. Oak Lawn certainly had the benefit of its privacy and its views, but for young Eleanor, it was the source of some very tough memories. Although it served as a childhood home, it never really felt like home to her—certainly not like Springwood felt to FDR.

Eleanor wrote about her time spent in this house in her autobiography, and once in a while, she would mention it in her My Day columns. In her writings, it sometimes seems as if she only wants to share the positive things, but then, almost reluctantly, she spills out some of the harsh memories as well. She spoke of how big the house was to her, with high ceilings and large bedrooms. She also mentioned that the house did not have electric or even gas and that they used lamps for light. There were nine master bedrooms and five servant rooms, with only two bathrooms to serve the entire household. Summers were spent in this house, where it could become dreadfully hot in the days before proper air conditioning, and Eleanor complained of wearing too many layers of clothing and how her fingers would stick to the keys on the piano when she practiced.[189]

The home was decorated "in the formal way," as Eleanor recalled, with marble fireplaces, candle chandeliers and a large beautiful library that had been mostly filled with her grandfather's religious books but was now filling with the novels that his rebellious children wanted to read. This library became a main focus in Eleanor's early years, as she longed to escape the real world. She took the books outside into the fields and read all day under the trees. Her grandmother only insisted that on Sundays no such books could be read—only scripture and hymns.[190] Church was still an important part for Grandmother Hall, and Eleanor could recall taking a carriage four miles down the road to St. Paul's Church in the village of Tivoli. The old church was built by the Livingston family in the 1860s, and it was no doubt painful for Eleanor to visit, as her mother and father were interred at the hall mausoleum just behind the church.

Mary Livingston Ludlow Hall was a widow when her grandchildren moved into her home. Her husband, Valentine, was a strict, religious man who had made the Bible and prayer part of everyday life. It was not a pleasant life for Mary, as her husband controlled every aspect of life and kept her in the dark when it came to financial decisions. Many of her children would rebel later in life, most likely because of what their father had put them through. When Valentine died at the age of forty-six in 1880, Mary was lost and unsure about how to manage the family's estate. She still had some of her own children living at home who needed to be dealt with, and it simply was not in her capacity to accomplish all of this alone. At first, Eleanor and her brother felt comfortable with their Hall relatives, who did their best to make them feel safe and help to ease the pain of the loss of their parents.[191]

Alcoholism was a common problem among many of Eleanor's relatives, including her uncles Valentine and Edward, who were living at Oak Lawn when Eleanor and Hall arrived. Although they were championship-winning tennis players and tried to help Eleanor with her horse-riding skills and tennis, their problems with alcohol and their antics, along with many other aspects of life at Oak Lawn, began to frighten Eleanor in her adolescence. Valentine and Edward would sit on the edges of the windows of the second floor and shoot at any visitors who came near the house. Eleanor kept three locks on her bedroom door to prevent her uncles from coming in whenever they pleased. She was even afraid of her governess, Madeleine, who appears to have tormented her. With so many things that made her uncomfortable,

The porch at Oak Terrace. *Franklin D. Roosevelt Library and Museum.*

there was at least a sense of belonging that came from Grandmother Hall. The care and attention that Mary bestowed on her young orphaned grandchildren was more than they ever properly received from their parents. Strangely, Eleanor found comfort in some of the servants in the household, like a washerwoman named Mrs. Overhalse who would let Eleanor help her with the washing.[192]

Interior of Oak Terrace. *Franklin D. Roosevelt Library and Museum.*

Later in life, Eleanor moved away from life at Tivoli, first for school in England, then with marriage and finally with her travels around the country and the world. Even in her busy schedule, though, she always found time to visit the house in Tivoli. Her grandmother died in 1919, and Eleanor wrote about her passing in her diary, saying she was "a gentle, good woman with a simple faith." As Eleanor traveled with Franklin from Washington to be with her Hall family members during their time of mourning, she considered whether or not her poor grandmother's life had been full enough: "If she had some kind of life of her own, what would have been the result?" Eleanor determined that she would try to live a more full and independent life than her grandmother had.[193]

Her aunt Maude Gray had begun using the house in the 1930s, but it was in terrible condition and would be for most of the later twentieth century. The home is now in private hands, and as of 2017, there has been an effort to restore the home for use in a manner fitting to Eleanor Roosevelt's legacy.

Part Three

ALBANY

SENATOR RENTALS

When FDR was elected as a New York state senator, his new political life included traveling regularly to Albany from Hyde Park or the townhouse in New York City. Today, we have the convenience of the New York State Thruway to make the trip easy and fast. For FDR, the fastest way to venture to Albany was to take the train from either Grand Central or Hyde Park station and then head north along the river. Just after his election, he received a letter from a friend and his cousin Ellen Delano's husband, Frederick Adams, who advised him about life in Albany. Adams informed him of the important clubs he should join: the Fort Orange Club and the Country Club. He advised him to do all of his banking at the Union Trust Company and attend church at St. Peter's. He went on to mention that he shouldn't waste time finding a house, as there would be a rush of senators looking for good real estate for rent.[194]

Over the course of the next few years as senator, the Roosevelts rented apartments around Albany. In 1911, FDR wrote in a diary entry, "We have rented the house of Mr. H. King Sturdee, No. 248 State Street for four months at $400 a month. We moved James and baby Elliott here from New York on Wednesday last and after returning to Hyde Park, brought Anna with us yesterday, Mama accompanying us." He went on to say that the house seemed "palatial after New York, and it is a comfort to have only three stories instead of six."[195] The family also stayed in the Ten Eyck Hotel, where they kept apartments for $45 a week. The Ten Eyck was known for its luxury and convenience to the capitol, which was an easy walk up the street.[196] At

A young FDR as state senator at his desk in Albany, 1911. *Franklin D. Roosevelt Library and Museum.*

this point in FDR's life, he still had the use of his legs, and his stride was long and fast-paced, as he undoubtedly considered the strides taken by his cousin Theodore years before. Meanwhile, Eleanor was enjoying running a household for the first time without the help of her mother-in-law. She found some form of independence in Albany that both she and Franklin enjoyed very much.[197] FDR would not be senator for long, as he was soon called to Washington, D.C., by Woodrow Wilson. His support for Wilson won him his dream job—a job once held by his cousin Theodore—assistant secretary of the navy.

The family left Albany for seventeen years, which would be some of the most challenging years for both Eleanor and Franklin. Between 1913, when FDR was sworn in as assistant secretary of the navy, and January 1929, when he took the oath of office as governor of New York State, much affected the lives of both Eleanor and Franklin. FDR had been shipped overseas during the Great War in an official capacity and saw war up close and personal, though not as close as those fighting it. When he returned in 1918, Eleanor discovered the heartbreaking letters that confirmed her suspicions of FDR's affair with Lucy Mercer. This discovery would forever change the dynamics of their marriage. In 1920, FDR ran alongside James M. Cox, who was running for president on the Democratic ticket. They lost the election to Warren G. Harding and Calvin Coolidge. In 1921, when he was only thirty-nine years old, Franklin contracted polio, which would leave him unable to walk. During the early 1920s, Eleanor found her voice and kept her husband's name circulating in the political world while he recovered in Warm Springs, Georgia.

It certainly appeared that FDR was content to focus on his rehabilitation as well as the care of other victims of paralysis when he made the purchase of the large ramshackle property that had become his haven. In 1926, he began the process of spending what would eventually amount to $200,000 to purchase 1,200 acres of land, thirteen little cottages and a rundown Meriwether Inn. It was over half of his personal wealth. It scared his mother, wife and political friends, but FDR was determined to make his Warm Springs Institute for Rehabilitation work for himself and for others. During this time, Eleanor stayed busy with her furniture company at Val-Kill, teaching at Todhunter School, writing and, of course, making sure that people did not forget the Roosevelt name in the Democratic Party. All of their work paid off when Governor Al Smith, who had been nominated to run for president, asked FDR to run for governor in 1928. FDR won his race by a very narrow margin, while Al Smith lost his.

GOVERNOR'S MANSION

O n New Year's Day in 1929, the Roosevelt family moved into their new home in Albany, the Executive Mansion. Al Smith and his family had called this house their home for eight years, and it wasn't anything like what the Roosevelt family had lived in before. Elliott Roosevelt, who was a teenager when they moved in, wrote that the mansion "seemed as if it might have been haphazardly assembled to serve as the classic house on haunted hill, popular in any number of Hollywood spine tinglers." He went on to explain the architecture: "Our new home showed obvious signs of paranoia in its confusion of turrets and towers, balconies and chimney stacks."[198] Elliott claimed that the Smith family had the interior furnishings and layout designed by a decorator from Bloomingdale's in New York, as if the house were a high-class New York hotel.

Eleanor got right to work overseeing the layout of the mansion, and like her son, she felt it wasn't quite home, but the house itself had seen a lot of change over the years. The Executive Mansion started as the private residence of Albany banker Thomas Olcott, who built the Italianate house in 1856. It didn't become the residence of a governor until it was rented in 1875 by Governor Samuel Tilden for a pricey $9,000 a year. Two years later, the state acquired the mansion for about $45,000 to serve as the permanent residence for New York governors. The mansion included greenhouses that were redone by Governor Charles S. Whitman during his administration from 1915 until 1919.

FDR, Eleanor, Elliott and John in the Governor's Mansion in Albany. *Franklin D. Roosevelt Library and Museum.*

Governor Al Smith was a great lover of animals, and he had a petting zoo added to the grounds during his time in office. But it was Smith who suggested that one of the three greenhouses be turned into a therapy pool for FDR. This is believed to be part of his way of convincing FDR to leave Warm Springs and re-enter public service. The idea of having a place to swim in warm waters while working on speeches and talking with journalists certainly enticed him. FDR announced his plans for the construction of the pool while at his home in Hyde Park on December 16, 1928. He argued that it was costing the state $6,000 a year to operate the greenhouses, which only managed to produce flowers worth some $750. Though the pool was not completed until 1929, FDR certainly took advantage of it during his time in office and his race to the presidency. During the Nelson A. Rockefeller era, the pool was filled in and returned to its greenhouse use while a new outdoor pool and tennis court were added. In 1988, Governor Mario Cuomo had the pool restored to just as FDR had it. It stands as a memorial to FDR today.[199]

Eleanor felt it was her duty to bring the house back down to earth. She saw to it that the Smith family took their zoo with them, which included "bear cubs, goats, six dogs, three monkeys, assorted elks, foxes, a raucous family of raccoons, and at least one tiger."[200] Up the grand

FDR's pool fully restored in the old greenhouse behind the Governor's Mansion. *Photo taken by the author.*

FDR listening to the radio inside the Governor's Mansion, 1932. *Franklin D. Roosevelt Library and Museum.*

FDR at his desk in the office of the Governor's Mansion, 1932. The chair where he sits is now in the living room at Springwood. *Franklin D. Roosevelt Library and Museum.*

staircase to the second floor was a large hall that the Roosevelts would use as a living room. There, FDR liked to set up a screen and projector to watch movies that he wasn't always able to get out and see.[201] Eleanor had chosen the largest room for him, and next door to him was a room for Missy LeHand. She worked side by side with him for many years and was absolutely devoted to him. This arrangement did not seem to bother Eleanor, since she had her own devoted group of friends. An electric elevator was installed in the building during FDR's tenure to accommodate his wheelchair. The elevator is still in use today. There was a staff of fifteen servants, which Eleanor felt was far too many, considering the state budget did not pay for them and the family had to foot the bill. Elliott recalled that his grandmother Sara was happy to assist in this matter.[202] The mansion is still used by current governors. Though it did suffer a fire during the Rockefeller era, it was quickly restored and houses a few treasures from the Roosevelts' four-year residency.

Notes

Chapter 1

1. Karl J. Valkenburgh, "Lambert Jochemse van Valckenburch of New Amsterdam," National Association of the van Valkenburg Family, https://navvf.org/lambert-manhattan.html.
2. Papers of Isaac Roosevelt, box 1, folder 3, Roosevelt Family Papers, Franklin D. Roosevelt Library, Hyde Park, New York (hereafter cited as Roosevelt Family Papers). A mention to the public of nominees to the Provincial Congress.
3. Ibid., box 1. Purchase of land in New York City, 1784.

Chapter 2

4. "LaGrange Terrace (Colonnade Row)," New York Architecture, http://www.nyc-architecture.com; Pieter Estersohn and John Winthrop Aldrich, *Life Along the Hudson* (New York: Rizzoli International Publications, 2018).
5. Laura Delano Household Accounts 1845–51, box 18, Delano Family Papers, Franklin D. Roosevelt Library, Hyde Park, New York (hereafter cited as Delano Family Papers).
6. Work at Lafayette Place, box 18a, Delano Family Papers.
7. Anna Eleanor Roosevelt, *The Autobiography of Eleanor Roosevelt* (New York: Da Capo Press, 1992), 47.

Chapter 3

8. Joseph Lash, *Eleanor and Franklin* (New York: W.W. Norton, 1971), 42.

9. "Mrs. Elliott Roosevelt Obituary," *New York Times*, December 9, 1892, https://timesmachine.nytimes.com/timesmachine/1892/12/09/104155489.pdf.

10. Roosevelt, *Autobiography of Eleanor Roosevelt*, 12.

Chapter 4

11. Ibid., 41.

12. Franklin Delano Roosevelt to Sara Delano Roosevelt, 1905, Roosevelt Family Papers.

13. Deborah Gardner, "Charles A. Platt in New York," in *Shaping an American Landscape, The Art and Architecture of Charles A. Platt* (Lebanon, NH: University Press of New England, 1995).

Deborah Gardner is an expert on the architecture of Charles A. Platt, and in this article, she explains some of his work in the Greater New York area. This article explains how he continued to use similar styles and designs in the houses he built off East Sixty-Fifth Street.

14. Roosevelt, *Autobiography of Eleanor Roosevelt*, 60.

15. *Upper East Side Historic District Designation Report*, Vol. 1 (New York: Landmarks Preservation Commission, 1981). This report was put together by a group of commissioners in NYC and contains the history of the architecture of the Upper East Side. It explains the changes made over the years and talks about the importance of the many different architects who left their marks there.

16. Blanche Weisen Cook, *Eleanor Roosevelt*, vol. 1 (New York: Viking, 1992), 228.

17. Deborah Gardner, *Roosevelt House at Hunter College: The Story of Franklin and Eleanor's New York City Home* (New York: Gilder Lehrman Institute of American History and Hunter College, 2009).

18. "Roosevelt House History," Roosevelt House Public Policy Institute at Hunter College, http://www.roosevelthouse.hunter.cuny.edu.

Chapter 5

19. Cook, *Eleanor Roosevelt*, Vol. 1, 297.

20. *New York Times*, March 28, 1942.

21. Eleanor Roosevelt, My Day, December 3, 1949.

22. Ibid., August 31, 1953.

23. Landmarks Preservation Commission Report, December 13, 1967.

24. Joseph Lash, *Eleanor: The Years Alone* (New York: W.W. Norton, 1972), 243.

25. William Turner Levy, *The Extraordinary Mrs. R* (New York: John Wiley and Sons, 1999), 54.

26. E. Roosevelt, My Day, December 2, 1959.

27. Edna Gurewitsch, *Kindred Souls* (New York: St. Martin's Press, 2002), 180.

28. Ibid., 181.

29. Lash, *Eleanor*, 237.

30. Levy, *Extraordinary Mrs. R*, 244.

31. E. Roosevelt, *Tomorrow Is Now* (New York: Penguin Books, 2012).

Chapter 6

32. Frederick Delano, *A Short Story of Algonac* (Newburgh, NY: Historical Society of Newburgh Bay and the Highlands, 1931).

33. Warren Delano to Franklin Delano, October 13, 1850, Delano Family Papers.

34. Ibid., June 8, 1851.

35. Ibid., June 26, 1851.

36. Andrew Jackson Downing, *Rural Essays* (New York: G.P. Putnam, 1858), xii.

37. Clara Steeholm and Hardy Steeholm, *The House at Hyde Park* (New York: Viking Press, 1950), 11.

38. Delano, *Short Story of Algonac*.

39. Algonac Diaries, Delano Family Papers, 150.

40. Delano, *Short Story of Algonac*.

41. Algonac Diaries, Delano Family Papers, 150.

42. Delano, *Short Story of Algonac*.

43. Ibid.

Chapter 7

44. Roosevelt Family Papers, box 4.

45. Ibid., box 1.

46. Ibid., box 23.

47. David Porter, *Biographical Dictionary of American Sports* (Westport, CT: Greenwood Press, 1995), 649–50.

Chapter 8

48. Ibid.

49. E. Roosevelt, *Franklin D. Roosevelt and Hyde Park: Personal Recollections of Eleanor Roosevelt* (Washington, D.C.: U.S. Government Printing Office, 1949).

50. Diary of Sara Delano Roosevelt, January 17, 1903, Roosevelt Family Papers.

51. Ibid., October 10, 1904.

52. Ibid., September 18, 1908.

53. Undated letter from Sara D. Roosevelt to FDR, Hyde Park, Roosevelt Family Papers.

54. "History of the Hyde Park Estate," President's Secretary's File, Subject File Hyde Park, Franklin D. Roosevelt Library, Hyde Park, New York (hereafter referred to Secretary's File, FDR Library). A piece that FDR started working on but never finished. However, he puts down the wrong date for the alterations to the house as 1912.

55. Letter from SDR to FDR, September 2, 1915, Roosevelt Family Papers.

56. Peggy Albee, *Historic Structure Report: Home of Franklin Delano Roosevelt* (Denver, CO: National Park Service, 1981), 69.

57. Deed between the Bennetts and FDR, September 5, 1911, Roosevelt Family Papers.

58. *Roosevelt Estate Historic Resource Study* (Hyde Park, NY: Home of Franklin D. Roosevelt National Historic Site, 2004).

59. Deed, Liber 454, Dutchess County Clerk, Poughkeepsie, NY, 426.

60. Letter from Mr. Plog to FDR 1935, Secretary's File, FDR Library.

61. Letter from FDR to Nelson Brown, March 17, 1939, Secretary's File, FDR Library.

62. E. Roosevelt, My Day, July 25, 1939.

63. Letter from Nelson Brown to FDR, January 11, 1944, Secretary's File, FDR Library.

64. Letter from FDR to Mr. Plog, December 12, 1941, Secretary's File, FDR Library.

65. E. Roosevelt, My Day, December 21, 1948.

66. Letter from FDR to James Townsend, June 14, 1941, Secretary's File, FDR Library.

67. Letter from Mrs. Moses Smith to FDR, October 24, 1938, Secretary's File, FDR Library.

68. Memo to Mrs. Nesbitt 1942, Secretary's File, FDR Library.

69. Janice Pottker, *Sara and Eleanor* (New York: St. Martin's Griffin, 2004), 333.

70. *Franklin D. Roosevelt Library: Hearing on H.J. Res. 268, a Joint Resolution to Provide for the Establishment and Maintenance of the Franklin D. Roosevelt Library*, 76th Cong. 13 (1939).

71. Cynthia M. Koch and Lynn A. Bassanese, "Roosevelt and His Library," *Prologue Magazine*, Summer 2001.

72. "Title III Franklin D. Roosevelt Residence," https://www.loc.gov.

73. "Roosevelt Deeded Estate to Nation," *Poughkeepsie Journal*, April 12, 1946.

74. "Thousands Visit Roosevelt Home," *Post Standard*, April 5, 1947.

75. "Roosevelt's Home Damaged by Fire," *New York Times*, January 24, 1982.

76. "Home of Franklin D. Roosevelt," National Park Service, https://www.nps.gov.

Chapter 9

77. Edward P. Newton, *Historical Notes of Saint James Parish* (Poughkeepsie, NY: A.V. Haight, 1913), 4.

78. Arnold Kopser, "A Brief History of St. James Church," St. James Episcopal Church, http://www.stjameshydepark.org.

79. Newton, *Historical Notes*, 56.

80. Ibid., 9.

81. Kopser, "A Brief History."

82. William B. Rhoads, "FDR Left His Mark on Nation and Area's Buildings," *Poughkeepsie Journal*, August 8, 1999.

83. Susan Quinn, *Eleanor and Hick: The Love Affair That Shaped a First Lady* (New York: Penguin Press, 2016), 345, 357.

84. This comes from conversations with various residents who lived in Hyde Park at the time. Kids walking home from Hyde Park Elementary and Regina Coeli School would stop by and see Hick at home. Rich Goring and Patsy Costello both remember seeing Hick in men's clothes.

85. Geoffrey C. Ward, *Before the Trumpet: Young Franklin Roosevelt* (New York: Harper and Row, 1985), 226.

86. Edmund P. Rogers to FDR, October 4, 1929, Roosevelt Family, Business, and Personal Papers, Franklin D. Roosevelt Library.

87. "Church Fire Suspicious," *Poughkeepsie Journal*, June 11, 1984.

88. Robert Klara, *FDR's Funeral Train: A Betrayed Widow, a Soviet Spy, and a Presidency in the Balance* (New York: Palgrave Macmillan, 2010), 150.

89. Recording from NBC News, April 15, 1945. Special thanks to Michael Dolan for sharing this with me.

90. Newton, *Historical Notes*, 59.

91. "Burial in Hyde Park Garden Next to Grave of Husband," *New York Times*, November 11, 1962.

92. "Somber Rites Contrast with Tireless Life Pace," *Poughkeepsie Journal*, November 11, 1962.

93. Ibid.

94. James Roosevelt II, Find a Grave, https://www.findagrave.com.

95. "Church Fire Suspicious," *Poughkeepsie Journal*, June 11, 1984.

Chapter 10

96. John F. Sears, *FDR and the Land: Roosevelt Estate Historic Resource Study* (Boston: Olmsted Center for Landscape Preservation, 2011), 223.

97. Kenneth S. Davis, *Invincible Summer: An Intimate Portrait of the Roosevelts Based on the Recollections of Marion Dickerman* (New York: Atheneum, 1974), 35.

98. Ibid.

99. Ibid., 45.

100. *Brooklyn Daily Eagle*, July 7, 1925.

101. Caroline O'Day, *Democratic Women's News*, November 1925.

102. The Personal Papers of Marion Dickerman, Franklin D. Roosevelt Library.

103. Davis, *Invincible Summer*, 46

104. Frank Futral, "Val-Kill Industries: A History," *Hudson River Valley Review* 26, no. 1 (Autumn 2009): 25.

105. Davis, *Invincible Summer*, 56

106. "Roosevelt Forced from Desk by Heat," *New York Times*, August 1, 1933.

107. Louis Torres, *Historic Resource Study* (Hyde Park, NY: Eleanor Roosevelt National Historic Site Val-Kill, 1980), 62.

108. Ibid., 50.

109. Ibid., 52.

110. Futral, "Val-Kill Industries," 26.

111. Ibid., 73.

112. Cook, *Eleanor Roosevelt*, Vol. 1, 332.

113. Torres, *Historic Resource Study*, 113.

114. Futral, "Val-Kill Industries," 34.

115. *New York Times*, May 14, 1936.

116. Cook, *Eleanor Roosevelt*, Vol. 1, 362.

117. Eleanor Roosevelt II, *With Love, Aunt Eleanor, Stories from My Life with the First Lady of the World* (Petaluma, CA: Scrapbook Press, 2004), 42.

118. Blanche Weisen Cook, *Eleanor Roosevelt*, Vol. 2 (New York: Viking, 1999), 525.

119. Ibid., 530.

120. Agreement between Nancy Cook, Marion Dickerman and Anna Eleanor Roosevelt, November 9, 1938, Secretary's File, FDR Library.

121. Interview with National Park Service security guard Gilbert Calhoun, Dutchess County Historical Society Yearbook, 2010, 84.

122. Nancy Cook to Eleanor Roosevelt, July 4, 1944, Eleanor Roosevelt Collection, Franklin D. Roosevelt Library.

123. Agreement between Eleanor Roosevelt, Nancy Cook and Marion Dickerman, August 25, 1947, deed 697, County Clerk's Office, Poughkeepsie, New York, 66.

124. Roosevelt Estate Historic Resource Study, Home of Franklin D. Roosevelt National Historic Site, 264.

125. *Poughkeepsie Journal*, January 6, 1950.

126. Levy, *Extraordinary Mrs. R*, 70.

127. The nameplate that still sits on Eleanor's desk was a gift and is spelled "Elanor Roosevelt."

128. Les Entrup interview, February 2, 1978, Roosevelt-Vanderbilt National Historic Site Oral History Collection.

129. Ibid.

130. Levy, *Extraordinary Mrs. R*, 69.

131. Ibid., 110. Marge was apparently quite amused by the fact that her dinner roll would appear on the front of the newspapers the following morning.

132. Ibid., 60.

133. Ibid., 73.

134. Roosevelt, *With Love, Aunt Eleanor*, 128.

135. Lash, *Eleanor*, 309.

136. Cultural Landscape Report for the Eleanor Roosevelt National Historic Site, Vol. 2, 2005, 131.

137. General Management Plan, Eleanor Roosevelt National Historic Site, May 1980.

138. "Eleanor Roosevelt," National Park Service, www.nps.gov.

Chapter 11

139. FDR, Memorandum, December 9, 1942, FDR Library.

140. Margaret Lynch Suckley to FDR, September 11, 1935, Wilderstein Historic Site Collections, Rhinebeck, NY.

141. Sears, *FDR and the Land*, 235.

142. *Poughkeepsie Journal*, November 14, 1938.

143. Geoffrey C. Ward, *Closest Companion: The Unknown Story of the Intimate Friendship between Franklin Roosevelt and Margaret Suckley* (Boston: Houghton Mifflin, 1995).

144. Letter from Henry Toombs to Marguerite LeHand, Secretary's File, FDR Library.

145. Adams-Faber Company Contract, June 1938, Secretary's File, FDR Library.

146. Adams-Faber Company letter to Missy LeHand, Secretary's File, FDR Library.

147. John G. Waite, *The President as Architect: Franklin D. Roosevelt's Top Cottage* (Albany, NY: Mount Ida Press, 2001), 47.

148. Ibid., 41.

149. Letter from Missy Lehand to Russell Linaka, October 24, 1939, Secretary's File, FDR Library.

150. *Life Magazine*, October 31, 1938.

151. Waite, *President at Architect*, 54.

152. Ward, *Closest Companion*, 272.

153. Ibid., 131.

154. Levy, *Extraordinary Mrs. R.*, 170.

155. Ibid., 172.

156. "Roosevelt's Phoneless Retreat Will Be Completed about Nov. 1: Dutchess Hill Cottage, Long 1-Story 'Dream House' Planned from President's Own Initialed Sketch," *New York Times*, October 9, 1938.

157. Waite, *President as Architect*, 61.

158. "The Dream House of Roosevelt Sold," *New York Times*, April 18, 1952.

159. *Poughkeepsie Journal*, March 20, 1966. Advertisement proclaimed that Val-Kill Heights was the place to look if you wanted to build a house in nice land close to schools.

Chapter 12

160. Ward, *Closest Companion*, 20.

161. Doris Kearns Goodwin, *No Ordinary Time, Franklin and Eleanor Roosevelt: The Home Front in World War II* (New York: Touchstone, 1994), 361.

162. "At Hyde Park: An Intimate Picture of the President at Home," *New York Times*, August 24, 1941.

163. David Byars, *Our Time at Foxhollow Farm, A Hudson Valley Family Remembered* (Albany, NY: SUNY Press, 2016), 115.

164. Adolf K. Placzek, *MacMillan Encyclopedia of Architects*, Vol. 3 (London: Free Press, 1982), 450–51.

165. *Building-Structure Inventory for Evergreen Lands* (Albany: New York State Office of Parks, Recreation, & Historic Preservation, 1987).

166. Ward, *Closest Companion*, 163.

167. Hazel Rowley, *Franklin and Eleanor: An Extraordinary Marriage* (New York: Farrar, Straus, and Giroux, 2010), 284.

Chapter 13

168. Carney Rhinevault and Shannon Butler, *Hyde Park in the Gilded Age* (Charleston, SC: Arcadia Press, 2019), 64.

169. Ward, *Closest Companion*, Preface.

170. Cynthia Owen Philip, *Wilderstein and the Suckleys* (Rhinebeck, NY: Wilderstein Preservation, 2001), 23.

171. *Historic American Buildings Survey* (Washington, D.C.: National Park Service), http://cdn.loc.gov.

172. Ward, *Closest Companion*, Preface.

173. "Biography of Fala D. Roosevelt," Franklin D. Roosevelt Presidential Library and Museum, https://www.fdrlibrary.org. Another excellent source is the biography of Fala: Daisy Suckley, *The True Story of Fala* (New York: Scribner, 1942).

174. Ward, *Closest Companion*, 237.

175. Obituary for Margaret Suckley, *New York Times*, July 2, 1991.

176. Ward, *Closest Companion*, 418. It is also possible that his last words were "be careful," as Laura Delano later claimed she heard him say this as they carried him from his desk to his bed in the lttle White House.
177. "Rescue on the Hudson: Dedicated Neighbors Fight to Save Wilderstein, the Unrestored Home of FDR's Former Archivist," *Historic Preservation* (July/August 1989).

Chapter 14

178. "The Descendants of John Jacob Astor," *New York Times*, 1898, https://timesmachine.nytimes.com.
179. Estersohn and Winthrop Aldrich, 188–90.
180. Steen Valetje Specifications, Estimates and Memoranda, 1848–50, box 30, Delano Family Papers, Franklin D. Roosevelt Library.
181. Ibid.
182. "Franklin H. Delano's Will," *Sun*, June 24, 1894.
183. *Poughkeepsie Daily Eagle*, June 22, 1985. Mentions Warren Delano using the house in Barrytown, spelled "Steinvalje," as his summer residence.
184. *New England Historical and Genealogical Register* (1921): LXXIX.
185. "The Walters Art Collection," *New York Times*, December 4, 1894.
186. "Warren Delano Killed by Train at Barrytown," *New York Times*, September 10, 1920.
187. Roosevelt, My Day, July 6, 1949.

Chapter 15

188. Clare Brandt, *An American Aristocracy* (New York: Doubleday, 1986), 25.
189. Roosevelt, *Autobiography of Eleanor Roosevelt*.
190. Ibid.
191. Cook, *Eleanor Roosevelt*, Vol. 1, 94.
192. Ibid.
193. Cook, *Eleanor Roosevelt*, Vol. 1, 249.

Chapter 16

194. Letter from Frederick Adams to FDR, November 9, 1910, Papers as NY Senator—Albany Residences, Franklin D. Roosevelt Library.

195. Diary of FDR, January 1–3, 1911, file 2, Papers as NY Senator—Albany Residences, Franklin D. Roosevelt Library.

196. Letter from the Ten Eyck Hotel, December 10, 1912, Papers as NY Senator—Albany Residences, Franklin D. Roosevelt Library.

197. Cook, *Eleanor Roosevelt*, Vol. 1, 202.

Chapter 17

198. Elliott Roosevelt, *An Untold Story: The Roosevelts of Hyde Park* (New York: G.P. Putnam and Sons, 1973), 269.

199. Interview with Stuart Lehman in the Executive Mansion, Albany, October 2019.

200. Cook, *Eleanor Roosevelt*, 394.

201. Elliott Roosevelt, *Untold Story*, 270.

202. Ibid.

ABOUT THE AUTHOR

S hannon Butler was born in Poughkeepsie and educated at local schools and universities. She began her career in museums by working at the Senate House State Historic Site in Kingston, New York. While there, she decided to go to college to pursue her passion for history, first attending SUNY Ulster, followed by SUNY New Paltz and finally earning her master's in history from SUNY Albany. She worked with the National Park Service at Roosevelt-Vanderbilt National Historic Sites for eight years, where she found her interest in Roosevelt history. In 2018, she became the town historian of the Town of Hyde Park and, a year later, was also made the historian of the Poughkeepsie Public Library. She is the co-author of *Hyde Park in the Gilded Age*. This is her first solo work.

CPSIA information can be obtained
at www.ICGtesting.com
Printed in the USA
BVHW020327091121
621088BV00021B/411